Night Flyer

SIGNIFICATIONS

Series editor
Henry Louis Gates, Jr.

Night Flyer

===

HARRIET TUBMAN
AND THE FAITH DREAMS
OF A FREE PEOPLE

TIYA MILES

PENGUIN PRESS   NEW YORK   2024

PENGUIN PRESS
An imprint of Penguin Random House LLC
penguinrandomhouse.com

LIBRARY OF CONGRESS CATALOGING-IN-PUBLICATION DATA
Names: Miles, Tiya, 1970– author.
Title: Night flyer : Harriet Tubman and
the faith dreams of a free people / Tiya Miles.
Description: New York : Penguin Press, 2024. | Series: Significations |
Includes bibliographical references and index.
Identifiers: LCCN 2023048092 (print) | LCCN 2023048093 (ebook) |
ISBN 9780593491164 (hardcover) | ISBN 9780593491171 (ebook)
Subjects: LCSH: Tubman, Harriet, 1822–1913. | Enslaved persons—
United States—Biography. | African American women—Biography. |
African Americans—Biography. | Fugitive slaves—United States—
History—19th century. | Underground Railroad.
Classification: LCC E444.T82 M55 2024 (print) | LCC E444.T82 (ebook) |
DDC 306.3/62092 [B]—dc23/eng/20240201
LC record available at https://lccn.loc.gov/2023048092
LC ebook record available at https://lccn.loc.gov/2023048093

Printed in the United States of America
1st Printing

Book design and Significations symbol by Daniel Lagin

For SDG, Harriet's biggest fan

And in loving memory of Steve McCullom

PROVOCATION:
GRASPING THE PAST IN THE PRESENT

Let us grasp the staffs of our past believing in their power
even now—

that we would be a people who meet desperation and sorrow

with a remembrance that protects us from despair.

—COLE ARTHUR RILEY, *BLACK LITURGIES*,
@BLACKLITURGIES, INSTAGRAM

———

Ours is the time of the seventh trouble. But we do not wait in these woods alone. Harriet walked this way before, showing us how the wilderness works. She could have leaned against that tree. She would have pointed out that star. She could have sketched a map in the dirt and bid us memorize it. Then she might have whispered a secret that the trees already knew:

We can be a flock alighting. If we join hands, we will fly.

———

COMPASS:
BECOMING THE FUTURE

On this path of becoming
Shrouded by hoot owl

White snake and nosy deer
callous feet muster creek

rock between toes that know
blisters cuts fourteen

and three babies people blue
black night brown limbs aching

amidst rusty leaves moses hushes
them up the mountain half her body

lost in the river the other in stars
her hands a basket her face grit

a young man guiding wife and child
through purple water looks over

his shoulder at the broken ones
in back ghosts rattling their bones

—QURAYSH ALI LANSANA, "PURGATORY,"
THEY SHALL RUN: HARRIET TUBMAN POEMS

CONTENTS

Preface

—

THE STORM

The trees themselves, as in winters past, will survive
their burdening,

broken thrive. And am I less to You,

my God, than they?

—ROBERT HAYDEN, "ICE STORM"

The storm was coming. She sensed its approach in the shift of the wind, the click-clack of branches, and the eddies of sea-moistened air. She craned her neck to view the sky, dark through a scaffold of winter-tree canopy. Wrapping her arms across her chest, she pulled her woolen shawl close, then knuckled one hand to her heart and curled the other around her revolver. Ever watchful of nature's signs, the woman waited. When the skies did part and the snow bore down in glassy shards, whiting out the silent scene of coastal forest, she may have felt the instinctual fear that all humans know in moments of heightened realization of their vulnerability to the elements. She might have trembled at the thought of what could befall her during the night—cold, hunger, even a kidnapping. Did she long to shut her eyes and pretend all was safety and sunshine around her? Did she want to turn and flee as splinters of wind-sharpened snow sped and spun? Did she ever ponder giving in, giving up? Most of us would. But that was not how Harriet Tubman's singular mind worked. Where others saw shut doors and unscalable brick walls, she dreamed into being tunnels and ladders. Submission to re-enslavement was not an option. And she did not face that storm alone.

On the December night in 1860 when Harriet Tubman found herself trapped by winter weather, she was making one of her final trips through the woods of Maryland's coastal plain to rescue stolen souls.[1] Their lives had been taken from them by a class of racial elites who feasted on the flesh of vulnerable people, turning the muscles of their victims' bodies, the children of their wombs, and the knowledge in their heads into long-term capital and short-term comfort. But these Black captives did not appear at the designated meeting place that night. So Harriet waited. Petite with a slender build and still limber in her late thirties, she pressed her back against the bark of a thick tree. This might have been a loblolly pine, the species that coated the old-growth forests along the Eastern Shore of the Chesapeake Bay. A companion to the stranded woman who stood barely five feet tall, that evergreen would have cast a net of protective crystalline needles.

Harriet's business in the woods was dangerous and secret. No detailed record was kept of her thwarted mission that night, but according to a supporter of the Underground Railroad who spoke to Tubman's first and only official biographer, Harriet Tubman told the snowstorm story to "a warmhearted, impulsive woman, who was engaged heart and hand in the Anti-Slavery cause." The story comes to us twice removed from Tubman's own lips, across a distance that exists in all published accounts of her life. Tubman told this listener that "for some unexplained reason" the people she was there to aid "did not come." As Tubman waited, "night came on and with it a blinding snowstorm and a raging wind. She protected herself behind a tree . . . and remained all night alone exposed to the fury of that storm."[2] Tubman took shelter against the tree's trunk, shivering through the evening as other warm-blooded creatures, like fox squirrels and snow geese, skittered, burrowed, or folded frigid, ice-tipped wings. What was it like to tuck into the dark depth of the winter woods? What was Tubman thinking as she shrunk beneath the branch-umbrella, listening for animal sounds behind the screech of the wind? Was she worrying about the fugitives who had not come yet, fearing the hunters trailing them and the trackers always searching for her? Was she turning over in her mind the cascade of events that had led her here to a test of her mettle and the silent company of this tree?

Less than a decade before, Harriet Tubman had herself been enslaved. But she had refused to die in her spirit for the benefit of the flesh market. She had found a life purpose anchored in her religious faith. For she believed it was God's intention that all people should live in freedom, and she ardently felt enlisted in this higher cause. "God's time is always near," she told a Northern friend in a dictated letter, "God set the North Star in the heavens; He gave me the strength in my limbs; He meant I should be free."[3] Harriet Tubman had come to believe that the God of her faith had not only ordained her liberation but also provided aid toward this end in the form of a lodestar and strong body. But Tubman (known in her childhood as Minty) had not come by this liberation theology easily or immediately. Her notion was radical in the mainstream society of her time that conceived of a God of social order and racial hierarchy. Her countercultural belief in a God of freedom stemmed from her lived experience, moral intuition, critical inquiry, cultural learning, religious feeling, and environmental surroundings. Through her openness to sources of knowledge that we might view as extraordinary today and her conviction that, with God's guidance, she had the power to alter outcomes, Harriet Tubman became formidable.

So when that "warm-hearted" woman who listened to

the snowstorm tale reacted this way: "Why, Harriet! . . . didn't you almost feel when you were lying alone, as if there was *no God?*"—she was fundamentally misunderstanding Harriet Tubman. For Harriet insisted she was not alone. God *was* with her. And it was in perilous places like this forest that she felt his presence most profoundly. "I just asked Jesus to take care of me," Harriet explained to the questioner, proclaiming that divine intervention had protected her from freezing that night.[4] Others who had braved the cold in search of freedom had not been so lucky. One "poor traveler" on the Underground Railroad in wintertime had been "severely frost-bitten" and died of lockjaw, the Black activist William Still recorded in his notes on the clandestine network around the year 1857. William Still noted in this same passage that the white activist Thomas Garrett had recently inquired about Harriet Tubman, worrying that she may have taken ill after an autumn rescue mission.[5] But Harriet had survived this scare in 1857, just as she had survived the storm in 1860. "'The Lord will provide' was her motto, and He never failed her," Harriet's colleague and first biographer wrote.[6]

Over the course of her long life, Harriet Tubman continuously professed this fundamental article of personal faith: God would take care. And just as God cared for her, she would spend a lifetime caring for others, trekking through the dark nights to deliver them from the evil that was slavery and creating sanctuary spaces in the North to receive them after hard journeys. By midlife, Tubman behaved much like the evergreen tree that had shielded her from the snowstorm in 1860, a partner of God on the earth who carried out an ethic of care with the aid of human and nonhuman allies.

It is apt that Harriet Tubman earned the byname Moses during her years as a freedom fighter. She sang songs with the lyrics "Moses go down in Egypt, Till ol[d] Pharo let me go" and sought to follow the God of the Christian Bible, even though she had never been taught how to read it in a land where it was illegal for slaves to learn the techniques of written word literacy.[7] She related to this biblical God intimately and imaginatively through prayer, dreams, aural inputs, visions, and the spoken or preached word. And Harriet Tubman's expansive yet specific version of the freedom-loving Judeo-Christian deity was not unique. She conceptualized God's personality in a manner commonly shared by the broader community of Black enslaved people. Theirs was a god of liberation as seen in the spectacular deliverance of the Jewish people from Egypt in the Old Testament stories. Black women in particular saw this god (gendered masculine in their time) as a caretaker as well as a liberator—fully present during their struggles, wholly invested in their survival, desiring their good quality of life, and inspiring hope for their future. This Black women's God of freedom and care was fiery and feeling, full of Old Testament Jehovah-style justice and New Testament Jesus-filled grace. He welcomed the rituals of Protestants and Catholics and recognized the echoes of West African faith practices. And his traits and deeds throughout time were captured in an "oral text" that enslaved African Americans shaped together "by extracting from the Bible or adding to biblical content those phrases, stories, biblical personalities and moral prescriptions relevant to the character of their life situation and pertinent to the aspirations of the slave community," the theologian Delores Williams has explained. "Passed down to black people through sermons, song, and public instructions," as the ethicist Renita Weems has put it, the enslaved community's Bible was spoken and heard more than read.[8]

Harriet Tubman lived her life based on this shared religious faith carried on the tongues of enslaved people. She knew the God of the oppressed both as an individual and as a member of a faith culture. And if we are to come closer to knowing *her*, we must recognize the centrality of her faith in the context of her vulnerability and in the development of her rebellious, antiestablishment character. Amid her extreme and continuous exposure to harm, Tubman felt, as the Harvard Divinity School scholar and associate dean Melissa Bartholomew has said about Black women believers writ large: "the safest place to be is in the will of God."[9]

Seeing Harriet Tubman as a faith-full woman first means revising some of the ways we have preferred to see her in histories and popular depictions: as a solitary figure, as a superhero, as a superhuman wielder of mysterious powers—a composite set of characteristics that reached a campy apotheosis in the comic representation of Harriet Tubman as a literal demon slayer.[10] While it is right that her roles as a heroic Underground Railroad conductor and a Civil War scout have been emphasized in books, films, and media (and, in the era before the culture-war campaign to scrub the history of slavery in some states, on grade school bulletin boards across the country), these representations veer toward superhuman portrayals that risk perpetuating a reductive image of Tubman expressed by some abolitionists, Northern neighbors, and academics in the nineteenth and early twentieth centuries—the Tubman who was impenetrably strange, with peculiarities and powers that are difficult to fathom or replicate. Intentionally or not, some of these observers portrayed Tubman as a racialized exotic, close to what we would now call the "magical Negro" trope. The antislavery advo-

cate Franklin Sanborn said of Tubman, "There is a whole region of the marvelous in her nature, which at times has
manifested itself remarkably . . . She is a negro of pure, or almost pure blood . . ."[11] Thomas Garrett, a key supporter of
Tubman's work and a committed Christian and abolitionist
himself, described her as a "noble woman, but a *black one,*
in whose veins flows not one drop of Caucasian blood" and
spoke of her "power of divination."[12] Helen Tatlock, an associate in New York, said of Tubman: "Harriet, when I knew
her in her matriarchal phase, was a magnificent looking
woman, true African, with a broad nose, very black, and of
medium height."[13] And Sarah Bradford, the author of two as-
told-to biographies that indelibly colored Tubman's image in
print, at times adopted a tongue-in-cheek tone at Tubman's
expense, writing that regarding Harriet "there seems but
one step from the sublime to the ridiculous" and asserting
that she was not "claiming any of [her] dear old friend Harriet's prophetic vision."[14] As Harriet Tubman's first biographer, Sarah Bradford conversed with Tubman often, published
remembrances that would yield funds for Tubman's mortgage and the support of people living under Tubman's roof,
brought her supplies, and lent her money. But Bradford also
demeaned Tubman as a hyperracial oddity, describing her as
"the black woman from the Southern states only two removes

from an African savage!"[15] Even W. E. B. Du Bois, an intellectual heavyweight who was, unlike the commentators above, African American himself, highlighted characteristics that rendered Tubman as an exotic, calling her "a full blooded African," and a "dark ghost," who exhibited "wild, half-mystic ways with dreams, Rhapsodies, and trances."[16]

The notion of a magical Tubman (minus the negative racialism and colorism) has its appeal even now, perhaps because in hindsight we know the evil that she was up against, and we desperately want to see her equipped to win her war against brazen inhumanity. But this quixotic picture painted by others also positions Harriet Tubman outside her family and community, outside a collective African American women's history, and beyond our reach as a potential, if imperfect, exemplar of how to resist oppressive systems and build supportive, life-sustaining communities. If we are to take serious stock of Harriet Tubman's journey on earth, we should strive to do so on her own cultural terms, seeing her "prophecies" and bold gambits to free others not as outlandish, bizarre, quaint, or innately racial, but as part of a religious worldview that foregrounded spiritual empowerment.

While Harriet Tubman did claim to know things that had not yet come to pass and did accomplish great feats of daring at her own personal risk, she acted out of a logic that made sense to her and would have made sense to other members of her Black female faith culture. The features of her character that some commentators saw as idiosyncratic were instead influenced by her multifaceted faith tradition, which combined Christian conviction with enslaved people's quest for justice, a belief in second sight, and the use of natural protections (like charmed roots and pouches of dirt and other sacred materials) based in West African, Native American, and Southern folk thought. Tubman's effectiveness in the material realm stemmed from her faith in a spiritual realm; it flowed from her mind, body, *and* spirit in communion with human and nonhuman beings. Attempting to grasp Tubman as a real person who lived and made difficult choices means studying her beliefs and ideas in cultural context. And as it turns out, Tubman was not only a practiced master of survival strategy but also a keen analyst of the natural and social worlds around her.

Harriet Tubman was one of a kind—singularly special *and* part of a cultural collective. Unique in nature and nurture in the way that every person is, she also shared a broader experience with captive Black women of the nineteenth century. While we cannot plumb the depths of her personality, due to the passage of time and limitations of the historical method, we can glean from extant sources that Tubman persistently demonstrated spiritual attunement, fluid intelligence, relational loyalty, emotional yearning, material longing, and aesthetic enjoyment—complex and at times competing characteristics filtered through her life experiences of love, loss, suffering, and illness. Harriet Tubman adored her parents. Harriet Tubman felt pain. She had a playful sense of humor. She loved fresh fruit and was particular about her clothing style.[17] She was also, in the words of the contemporary historian and biographer Deirdre Cooper Owens, "fragile and in need of gentle care."[18] And every time she entered the woods to rescue someone else from slavery, Tubman did so as a real woman who felt that God held her hand. Picturing her huddled beneath a tree during a cold December night, determined to stand firm despite not knowing what would happen next, and recognizing that she acted out of a complex worldview held in common with other Black women and enslaved people, resizes Tubman the cultural icon to human scale and expands our faith in the human capacity to collectively weather life's storms.

There is a version of Harriet Tubman that we love to love—the woman, in the words of a great-grandniece of Tubman, Judith Bryant, "slogging through swamps at night, and all." But as Bryant wisely said, this "mythic" legend collapses into a "mini story . . . this little story of courage," due to reduction and repetition. "Yeah she did all that, but to me there's a bigger significance of what that really means in today's world," Bryant said.[19] By turning Tubman into a superhero with vague "woo-woo" powers, we diminish her in memory and reduce our capacity to learn from her life. This simplistic superwoman-of-the-swamps myth obfuscates at least two critical elements of Harriet Tubman's character: who she was on the inside and how she saved lives. Peeling back the layers of myth, to the best of our ability, begins to reveal her values and methods. What principles did Tubman live by? And what tactics did she swear by? This book explores both questions with an emphasis on two themes central to Tubman's worldview: spirituality (her belief in God, heaven, and unseen powers) and ecology (her belief in the integrity and import of relationships among all natural beings). These twin tenets of belief converged in Tubman's life to shape a practice of being in the world best captured by the term luminous pragmatism.[20]

Before I started on this quest to trace the lifeline of Harriet Tubman, I, too, had fallen for the static image of Tubman as superwoman. Her bravery, though laudable, seemed to come prepackaged in a box of stock stories and folksy sayings. I realize now, and with chagrin, that she had become a stock figure in my imagination, a known hero in the cast of characters that we might call the abolitionist avengers. But as I paused in the moments and places where Harriet herself stopped to plan and to pray, I began to see more clearly the woman behind the cardboard cutout. She was startlingly spiritual and eerily smart. She saw more than she let on and knew more than we have recognized. By the time I made my way to her burial plot at the end of my research journey, I felt I was in the presence of a guru for her time and ours.

I see compelling reasons for retelling Tubman's story now, in the 2020s, and for suggesting that her life narrative, in many ways familiar, still holds surprises for us. When Judith Bryant did an interview for a Maryland State Parks oral history project in 2011, she stressed that "we seem to be . . . losing our coherence in this country," and that as an antidote to dissolution, we should "look again at all of our heroes." It is stating the obvious to note that the national status quo has deteriorated dramatically since Bryant made this comment. Still, Tubman's era—the nineteenth century—was worse. She matured into her calling as an unfree Black woman during a period of racial brutality, masculinist primacy, chaotic change, political splintering, and impending civil war. Yet during that time of crisis, "she got things done," as Bryant crisply put it. Harriet Tubman was heroic, but she was not a superhero beyond the reach of our understanding, identification, and compassion. We need not hold her at so great a distance that she becomes a blur. "She's over there. But she

Harriet Tubman holding a rifle and wearing a striped skirt
and jacket, with a satchel over her shoulder. The setting is
a Civil War encampment, circa 1863–68. Frontispiece of Sarah
H. Bradford's *Scenes in the Life of Harriet Tubman*, 1869.

Courtesy of Harvard University Fine Arts Library. National Portrait Gallery,
Smithsonian Institution, open access.

ought to be here. And we ought to be here with her," Bryant
concluded.[21]

A flesh-and-blood woman of her antebellum age, Harriet Tubman lived a perilous life with profound lessons for
ours. Tubman was no nihilist. She believed in the possibility

of brighter futures, and she acted on those visions. She put faith in God, had faith in nature, and kept faith with all sorts of people. Even so, she made grave mistakes and suffered real harms while gathering over ninety years of wisdom. If we are now living in "the time of the seventh trouble," as Tubman might well have deemed it, what route would she advise us to take through this wilderness?

Night Flyer

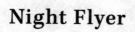

Introduction

—

THE WAY

I felt all the while that I was sustained by some invisible power.

—ELIZABETH, *MEMOIR OF OLD ELIZABETH*, 1863

It seemed as if I heard my God rustling in the tops of the mulberry-trees.

—ZILPHA ELAW, *MEMOIRS OF THE LIFE,*
RELIGIOUS EXPERIENCE, MINISTERIAL TRAVELS
AND LABOURS OF MRS. ZILPHA ELAW, 1846

The Lord was pleased to give me light and liberty among the people.

—JARENA LEE, *THE LIFE AND RELIGIOUS EXPERIENCE*
OF JARENA LEE, A COLOURED LADY, 1836

Harriet Tubman's wooden cradle appears early in this tale, but you will not find a cradle-to-grave biography here. Excellent traditional biographies (referenced throughout this book) chronicle the range of events, relationships, and historical contexts that made up this famous woman's consequential life. The focus of my biographical take—Harriet Tubman's eco-spiritual worldview—stems from Tubman's baseline principles as revealed in her self-representations. Because Tubman did not read or write, maintaining this focus is tricky. The words she spoke and beliefs she held that remain available to us now were filtered through the minds of other people—typically white, middle-class, antislavery women who recorded her speech and told her story, like Sarah Bradford, Tubman's first biographer. The reportage of these reform-minded women who thought of themselves as promoting Tubman does have value for this study and will be plentifully present. At the same time, there exists another, often overlooked group of women whose pages yield just as much, if not more, insight into Tubman's motivations and reasoning. To better understand Tubman while centering the theme of her belief, this book draws on the life stories of similar women—bold historical figures who considered themselves to be Black, female, and holy in the nineteenth century.

The classic tradition of African American women's spiritual narratives consisting of a handful of memoirs written or dictated by Black women evangelists gives us access to their lives and inspires the format of this book. The most widely read of these texts today is the earliest: *The Life and Religious Experience of Jarena Lee*, first published in 1836. Zilpha Elaw (in 1846), Old Elizabeth (in 1863), and Julia A. J. Foote (in 1879) also told their stories of religious devotion during the slavery, Civil War, and Reconstruction eras.[1] Together, their memoirs help to shade in interior facets of Tubman's life; and her life, in turn, illuminates the experiences of these lesser-known women.

I first came across the genre of Black women's spiritual narratives three decades ago, when I was a new graduate student immersed in the study of African American women's early print culture. I published my first essay in an academic periodical, the *Journal of the Interdenominational Theological Center*, after realizing that one-hundred-plus years after their publication, these texts still spoke to me intellectually and personally. My essay drew primarily on the language of the itinerant preacher Elizabeth to address women's marginal status as "speckled birds" in the Black church of the 1990s. I wrote the piece as a young woman in my twenties who had been raised in a Black Baptist church in Ohio and then had gone off to college in Massachusetts, learned about feminist ideas in the then recent works of bell hooks and Alice Walker, and started questioning what I had come to view as insensitive and unjustified male authority in my home congregation. In my master's degree program in Women's Studies, I explored what I felt was a clash between faith and feminism by taking a course in womanist theology (see the Note on Process and Sources at the end of this book for more on "womanism") and identifying early Black women spiritual leaders who followed what they identified as God's call to preach even when male church leaders dissuaded and harassed them. Back then, I read these narratives as spiritual accounts of African American women coming to Christian (usually Methodist) faith, being transformed, feeling God's power, discerning God's will, and preaching the gospel. I also saw these life stories as trenchant social criticism of the imbalances of power between women and men, the enslaved and the free. My view of the value of these memoirs and of their dual character as spiritual and political accounts has not changed, even as my personal thoughts about Christianity, agnosticism, atheism, and meditation have traversed peaks, plains, and valleys. In returning to these narratives now, as a way of reframing Harriet Tubman that rings true to my sense of her persona as evident in the historical record, I notice that these testimonies also include subtle content about the relationship between Black women prophets and their environments. These holy women communed with God not only in their minds and spirits but also in isolated places that were often located in natural surrounds.

Each of these Black female spiritual writers who lived and published during Harriet Tubman's lifetime—Jarena Lee, Zilpha Elaw, Old Elizabeth, and Julia A. J. Foote— struggled with varying forms of captivity and constraint, including legal enslavement in the South, bound servitude in the North, mental illness, physical illness, bodily disability, and male authority over their lives. And each experienced a wrenching renewal of individual consciousness and purpose through a relationship with the god of her belief as a prerequisite and mandate for doing the seemingly impossible: challenging entrenched social systems of racial and gender subjugation at the risk of her own safety, health, and

social acceptance. These women who came to view themselves as "sanctified," or "holy" after an emotionally wrought
process of spiritual transformation, formed a vanguard of
mental defense against the corrupting presence of slavery
in both spiritual and earthly realms. They believed in
God's power to set souls "at glorious liberty," as Zilpha Elaw
phrased it, and they saw God as intensely democratic in this
aim. The God of their belief sought to set all souls free from
sin and would call women as well as men, Blacks as well as
whites, to spread this gospel. Foregrounding God's democratic character, the memoir of Elizabeth (for whom no surname is given in the text) begins with an epigraph from
Scripture: "There is neither Jew nor Greek, there is neither
bond nor free, there is neither male nor female, for ye are all
one in Christ Jesus."[2] Jarena Lee opened her memoir with
the biblical line "And it will come to pass . . . that I will pour
my Spirit upon all flesh; and your sons and your *daughters*
shall prophecy," italicizing the word *daughters* to underscore
her argument about women's right to preach. And Julia
Foote insisted midway through her account in which being
"colored," female, and young disqualified her from leadership
in the eyes of many church members: "God is no respecter of
persons."[3]

These women were adamant about spreading their message. Jarena Lee preached in the North and the South and

once commented on a man "who was a great slaveholder, and had been very cruel" coming twice to hear her preach in New Jersey.[4] Lee as well as Zilpha Elaw preached on the Eastern Shore of Maryland, where a young Harriet Tubman may have heard their words.[5] Elizabeth preached in Maryland, too, and was almost arrested, probably in the metropolis of Baltimore, when she warned of the judgment in store for "the city" that rebelled against God. About her avoidance of arrest, Elizabeth wrote, "The Lord delivered me from their hands." In Virginia, Elizabeth "spoke against slavery" directly, and when threatened with imprisonment said to her accusers: "If the Lord had ordained me, I needed nothing better."[6] These fiercely religious Black women, who upheld freedom (of soul, mind, and body) as well as democracy as divine values, were Harriet Tubman's temporal contemporaries and cultural kin. They all shared what the anthropologist of religion T. M. Luhrmann has called a "faith frame" and practices for "kindling" belief that made the divine or spiritual presence "feel more real."[7] Together, their lives form a tapestry of social bravery rooted in a fully felt, richly interpreted, environmentally informed faith tradition.

In the fashion of these nineteenth-century spiritual memoirs that overlap with the slave narrative genre in the African American women's literary canon, the story I tell of Harriet Tubman's life is principally an account of her faith journey, in which she awakens to a sense of the sinful world and her place in it, joins with a spiritual force that she identifies as God/Jesus, comes into an awareness of her God-given capacities to challenge slavery, and "preaches" a gospel of freedom through spoken words and radical actions in various environments. For Tubman, slavery was an evil, and religious awakening was also a political awakening as she realized that the God of her heart and community championed liberation. She stood among peers who believed liberation had "spiritual and social dimensions" with the purpose of "restor[ing] a sense of self as a free person and as a spiritual being," as the ethicist Emilie Townes has put it.[8]

Important, too, in the Black women's faith culture that Tubman practiced, was God's work in and through nature. Tubman's relationship with God and her pursuit of his will unfolded in living ecological contexts—upon and among the changing lands, waters, and residents of the natural world— South and North. Tubman observed, understood, and accessed these natural features and creatures, often enlisting them in her freedom crusade. In this aspect, too, she shared a sensibility with other Black spiritual women who sought out God beneath trees, in agricultural fields, and among livestock whom they viewed as sentient. Their cognizance of nature's role in the world was sophisticated, reflecting what the environmental literary critic Kimberly Ruffin has termed the "ecological burden-and-beauty paradox." These women were fully aware of how land and water could figure as spaces of exploitation in the context of enslavement and servitude *and* of the potential for these features of nature to provide sustenance or refuge. As the environmental historian Dianne Glave has declared: "African Americans have long envisioned the environment in luminous and evocative ways, while at the same time remaining pragmatic and realistic about the wilderness." For Tubman and these holy women, nature, though capricious, melancholic, and potentially perilous, could also be counted among God's allies.[9]

Harriet Tubman is arguably the most famous Black woman ecologist in U.S. history, although she has not traditionally been viewed that way. She was a student of organisms (human and nonhuman), habitats, and interrelationships. Her sources of strength and information were as much natural as they were "supernatural." And more than that, her "repeated journeys into slaveholding America" required "ecological confidence," in the words of Kimberly Ruffin.[10] She studied the elements of nature around her, connecting with plants, trees, animals, and stars, until she became, as Angela Crenshaw—a former ranger at the Harriet Tubman Underground Railroad State Park and currently acting superintendent of Maryland State Parks—has put it, "the ultimate outdoors woman."[11]

Tubman depended on nature as a symbolic conduit of God's messages and a material provider of care and aid. We can learn from her embrace of this tie between faith and environment. As much as today's climate justice activists may need the lights of faith and hope to fuel them through the days of shock and deep adaptation that may lie ahead, Christian adherents who might admire the rock-solid religious faith espoused by Tubman should notice, too, how her discovery and enactment of what she understood to be God's will depended on intact ecosystems. These environments were changing slowly due to organic processes while being drastically altered by human economic development even then. Nevertheless, the forests and tributaries, sediment and coastline of the mid-1800s were stable enough to provide context and cover for Tubman's spiritual and political liberation.[12]

It is worth our notice, too, that efforts to conserve vulnerable patches of Eastern Shore land, as climate change erodes clay-rich ground and commercial development gobbles up acreage, link directly to our opportunity to better understand Harriet Tubman. In 2020, the U.S. Fish and Wildlife Service purchased a 2,600-acre parcel next to the existing Blackwater National Wildlife Refuge, south of the city of Cambridge, Maryland. The aim was to extend the refuge's footprint, which was shrinking in other areas due to sea level rise. The manager of the wildlife refuge, Marcia Pradines, invited archaeologists to search the newly acquired terrain for the home of Harriet Tubman's father, who she had heard from local residents might have lived in the area. An archaeologist working with Maryland's Department of Transportation, Julie Schablitsky, answered the call and found a site now identified as the Ben Ross cabin.[13] The discovery of Tubman's father's homeplace as a result of a conservation pitch made in an effort to outpace climate destruction has opened a window into Tubman's youth. Environmental protection can aid historical investigation even as our interpretations of the past are enriched by attending to ecological meanings in the lives of historical figures we thought we knew.

And as much as Harriet Tubman's spiritual worldview was inherently communal, political, and environmental, it was also intellectual. What Tubman experienced as God-given revelations about the unjust order of her social world were simultaneously outpourings of her own fertile mind. Tubman was a political visionary because of her strong faith *and* because she drew on remarkable intellectual strengths. She became practiced at reading people as well as landscapes, and she was capable of picturing possible futures that contradicted present realities. By the time she reached adulthood, Tubman was a master of observation, interpretation, and misdirection. "She was a trickster and a disguise artist," the Reverend Paul Gordon Carter, longtime guide at the Harriet Tubman Home in Auburn, New York, says on his tours. When Tubman's associate Ednah Dow Cheney wrote the following about Tubman: "She is a rare instance, in the midst of high civilization and intellectual culture, of a being of great native powers, working powerfully, and to beneficent ends, entirely unaided by schools or books," Cheney was steeped in a mainstream nineteenth-century culture skeptical of Black intelligence. Nevertheless, Cheney's couched words do reveal a fact about Tubman discernible to those who knew her and less remarked upon in our time: Harriet Tubman possessed a sharp intellect characterized by a radical range of thought and deep repository of knowledge that could equip her from the tobacco field to the battlefield. She was, as the environmental sociologist Dorceta Taylor has noted, a font of "ecological knowledge and awareness," and, as the astronomer Chanda Prescod-Weinstein has phrased it, a holder of "Black cosmological knowledge."[14] She made choices based on a trove of thought that we can still glimpse through the limited oral histories, written records, biographical descriptions, and physical landscapes that survive her time. Tubman's keen insights, social critiques, and proposed solutions to her society's worst problems—chattel race slavery, civil war, entrenched poverty, and women's subjugation—are hidden in plain sight among the fragments of her recorded songs, sayings, and speeches and in the secondhand accounts of her actions. Within her imperfectly preserved words and deeds lie the imprints of her ideas. After a traumatic head injury impacted her cognitive functions when she was young, Tubman continued to evaluate local conditions and social interactions with a neuro-atypical mind fused to a sensitively attuned spirit and informed by studied attention to nature.

Harriet Tubman often appears alongside Frederick Douglass in our national memory of abolitionist heroes, the female yin to his male yang. But while Douglass is heralded for lithe orations and sophisticated writing, Tubman is more often represented as a doer, not a thinker. Rarely do we see her referenced in lineages of Black intellectuals as a forebear to creative geniuses like Audre Lorde, Angela Davis, Alice Walker, or Toni Morrison. But Harriet Tubman's activist agenda did reflect a core concept—the notion that freedom was for everyone and that Black women, among the most oppressed, could lead the way to liberation. The boldness of Tubman's freedom theorem, and her willingness to risk her life to defend it, inspired theorists who came after her, including the Black feminist organizers of the Combahee River Collective, who named their group and their now famous 1977 statement after the place where Tubman enacted her core concept at scale, and a host of Black women theologians who have adopted Alice Walker's term *womanist* to categorize their intellectual tradition.

All that remains of Harriet Tubman's self-reportage (written down by others) tells us she oriented to the world from a place of immersive religious belief—an experiential space of integration between what she knew and what she felt, between rational thought, intuition, spiritual sensation, and landscape awareness. Her holistic belief system is partly visible to us now through the written repository of her prayers, songs, and dreams. Among the best preserved of Tubman's speech acts are her prayers, which appear throughout early biographies. Prayer was a space of convergence among these subjective modes (feeling, sensing, thinking) for Tubman. She processed her many dilemmas through prayer. Indeed, praying is a form of deep thinking, or, as the anthropologist Luhrmann has expressed it, "prayer is an act of thinking about thinking" that causes people to "attend to their own thoughts."[15] When Tubman prayed, she was not only pouring her heart out to God; she was also problem-solving. In addition to prayers, the spirituals Tubman sang are relatively well preserved and indicate intriguing lines of thought. When Tubman chose a hymn to sing, she was scrolling through a jukebox in her mind, selecting the right words and rhythms for the circumstance. These spirituals functioned like sermons for her, like exhortations or sets of instructions. Tubman often sang as a way of communicating with others, vocalizing her analysis of the state of human and divine affairs and transmitting concrete action plans.

While prayer and song were thought forms that Tubman engaged when awake, dreams expressed her mind at work while she was semiconscious in sleep. She seems to have been plagued by frightening dreams since childhood. These dreams worsened following the head injury that she suffered at the hands of an overseer during adolescence, after which Tubman endured what scholars conclude were seizures caused by temporal lobe epilepsy (or TLE). During and perhaps preceding these seizures, Tubman sometimes saw visions, a symptom shared by others with TLE. Her visions projected spiritual imagery onto the screen of her mind and may have been accompanied by strong feelings of religiosity. While neurological research has not yet uncovered all the ways that epileptic seizures affect the brain, scientists have found that seizures likely impact dreams during sleep and certainly spur waking visions, or sightings of light, sounds, and scenes accompanied by unusual feelings often referred to as "epileptic auras." People living with temporal lobe epilepsy can experience daytime seizures that propel them into a "dreamy state," during which images from nighttime dreams can sometimes reappear. And while sleeping at night, they can have dreams that are influenced by seizures, such that the physical symptoms of a seizure become part of the dream, or, more rarely, these dreams may turn into nightmares accompanied by feelings of dread and fear.[16] The workings of Harriet Tubman's mind were more complex than we know, shaped by her natural intelligence and affected by her changed neurological condition. Her prayers, songs, dreams, and visions were all configurations and expressions of her thought processes, conscious or semiconscious. They were, in other words, productions of Tubman's beautiful mind inflected by her spiritual sensibility, her exposure to religious iconography, and her medical condition.

Tubman's visionary turn of mind, enhanced by religious faith and by a debilitating brain injury, had been formed partly through adversity and accident. Even so, the quality of her dreams and visions, represented as prophetic by Tubman herself and by her peers, was not unique. The other Black "holy" women described here also heard voices, saw visions, had fainting spells or blackouts, communed with spirits they took to be God, Jesus, or angels, and acted on these experiences in ways that sometimes shocked their contemporaries. (And beyond this specific racial and gendered demographic, prominent leaders of rebellions and escapes from slavery, like Nat Turner, a Black man from Virginia, and Laura Smith Haviland, a white woman from Michigan, also described prophetic dreams.) While acknowledging Tubman's intellectual gifts and personal story of trauma, we can note that she was not alone in her fierce convictions or dramatic actions. Instead, she shared the company of a cohort of Black women who all knew some form of captivity, believed themselves to be spiritually empowered, and embraced freedom as a core tenet of their Christian faith.

We can gain a more concrete sense of the multidimensional belief system held by Tubman and members of her faith culture by considering the representation of another iconic enslaved Black woman—the fictional mother and grandmother, Baby Suggs, crafted by Toni Morrison in her Pulitzer Prize–winning novel of slavery, *Beloved*. Like Harriet Tubman, the character Baby Suggs is an emotionally and physically scarred survivor of Southern slavery who gravitates toward natural environments and loves the beauty of colorful cloth. Baby Suggs is also a lay spiritual leader who preaches about Black feelings, bodies, and right to life in a sunlit clearing in the woods beyond her Ohio home. Morrison writes of Baby Suggs:

> When warm weather came, Baby Suggs, holy, followed
> by every black man, woman and child who could make
> it through, took her great heart to the Clearing—a wide-

open place cut deep in the woods nobody knew for what at the end of a path known only to deer . . . In the heart of every Saturday afternoon, she sat in the clearing while the people waited among the trees.

After situating herself on a huge flat-sided rock, Baby Suggs bowed her head and prayed silently. The company watched her from the trees. They knew she was ready when she put her stick down. Then she shouted, "Let the children come!" and they ran from the trees toward her.[17]

There in the Clearing made sacred through religious practice, Baby Suggs calls the children to laugh, the men to dance, and the women to cry, urging them to express deep feeling through sound and movement, "until, exhausted and riven, all and each lay about the Clearing damp and gasping for breath. In the silence that followed, Baby Suggs, holy, offered up to them her great big heart."[18]

The spiritual wisdom of Baby Suggs, her combined perception and prescription bound up in faith and nature, captures the essence of Tubman's Way—a path of spiritual belief, political conviction, and philosophical thought expressed through word (storytelling and song) and action (flight and caretaking) within and together with nature (God's creation). And in walking this Way, Harriet Tubman was an inheritor, participant, and cocreator of a powerful survival practice built from Black women's phenomenological experience. In the midst of prolonged crisis that might be called a personal and political "wilderness," Tubman honed mental tools of preparation and navigation.

Harriet Tubman's story unfolds in these pages as a sequence of faith seasons, the phases of her religious growth intertwined with her intellectual and political development. I follow her from the spring of her youth to the winter of her wisdom years by relying on her as-told-to accounts and dictated letters, the lyrics of her spiritual songs, descriptions by people who knew her, newspaper accounts, slave narratives, spiritual memoirs, published scholarly biographies, exchanges with Tubman experts, oral histories, and a method of dream mapping that draws links between the images and vocabulary of her dreams and symbolic as well as ecological associations. I find, above all, that Tubman's belief in a freedom-loving, caretaking God was both a concept and conveyance, carrying her through the woods and the storms and empowering her delivery of hundreds of souls from ghost lands to free lands.

But even as religious belief was the bedrock of Harriet Tubman's personal power, this power came with moral complications and at personal cost. "Whenever a saviour emerges, there are bound to be problems," the historian

Harriet Tubman standing in a long skirt and button-down top.

Photo by Harvey B. Lindsley, in Auburn, New York, circa 1871–76. Collection of the Smithsonian National Museum of African American History and Culture shared with the Library of Congress, open access.

Sharony Green has wryly observed.[19] This was true of Tubman, who addressed ethical dilemmas in ways that may disturb us in retrospect. She was at times reckless in her actions and embraced violence as a tactic for achieving what she saw as righteous ends and defending those she loved. As William Still, a comrade in the struggle, put it: "She had a very short and pointed rule or law of her own, which implied death to any who talked of giving out or going back." Just as Tubman was willing to bully those in her charge, she showed little interest in what is now called "self-care." She ran her body into the ground, refusing self-protection, rest, and recovery. Tubman "seemed wholly devoid of personal fear," William Still wrote. "While she thus manifested such utter personal indifference, she was much more watchful with regard to those she was piloting."[20] Harriet Tubman behaved like a person bent on self-sacrifice. Indeed, she said she was content to die when God no longer had use for her, which raises an uncomfortable question about the value she placed on her own life. And while Tubman was a champion for Black people, the record is fuzzy on her relations with Indigenous people in the places where she lived. Knowingly or not, she built her Black sanctuary community in New York on land forcibly taken from Cayuga people of the Haudenosaunee Confederacy during the American Revolutionary era. If Tubman was a freedom prophet, she was also a religious zealot—a true believer in a god and a cause, willing to sacrifice all for both.

Sketching in both light and shade, I offer a portrait of Harriet Tubman, the fierce dreamer and fragile leader of a people who refused to be ghosted. Called Moses by her followers, she was one among many wilderness walkers who crafted an epic, yet imperfect, culture of resilience.

1

THE WATER

Wade in the water
Wade in the water, children
Wade in the water
God's going to trouble the water.

—"WADE IN THE WATER,"
TRADITIONAL SPIRITUAL

In a world like this, what can faith mean?

—JOANNA MACY, "FAITH, POWER,
AND DEEP ECOLOGY," 1991

To be taken is surely every child's nightmare. The boogeyman, the ghoul in the shadows, or the monster underneath the bed haunts the edges of tender minds, breaking through in the darkness. For Minty Ross, the girl who would one day become Harriet Tubman, that boogeyman was a demon called Slavery, and his powers to snatch children from the ones who loved them was tangibly, terribly real.[1] She arrived in a world drenched in threat and neglect. These powerfully negative twin forces shaped her early consciousness, imparting an indelible sense of insecurity, shame, and purpose.

When Minty Ross was born around the year 1822, she entered a family shredded by the teeth of the demon Slavery.[2] Her mother, Rit, and father, Ben, were each enslaved by different owners on the coast of the vastest estuary in the United States. These swelling shores and fertile lands that had long been home to Nanticoke, Choptank, and many other Indigenous peoples composed the Chesapeake Bay of eastern Maryland.[3] Rit, whose full name was Harriet Green, had herself been born in the late 1780s to an African woman called Modesty, who had suffered the original break from kin during the Middle Passage when she was brought to this place from her home in the belly of a slaving ship. If Modesty arrived in Maryland in the 1770s, she may have come from Senegal, as ships originating from that French-colonized West African nation appear in a database of such voyages. Modesty conceived Rit with a man whose name has eluded historical records. Some historians suppose that this man may have been Modesty's enslaver. Rit had siblings who also entered the world behind a shroud of racial mystery.[4]

Rit Green and Ben Ross were each conceived in states of bondage. Their ultimately loving marriage was as well. When Rit's legal owner, Mary Pattison Brodess (who had obtained Rit from her Pattison family line), remarried to the well-off entrepreneur and timber exporter Anthony Thompson after her first husband, Joseph Brodess, died, she moved some of the people she owned to Thompson's plantation. Rit and Ben were then residing in physical proximity on the Thompson estate, a large property of field, forest, and marshy

Water, sky, land, and loblolly pine trees in Cambridge, Dorchester County, Maryland. Notice the large eagle's nest tucked into a center pine. This marshland scene was captured near Key Wallace Drive and Wildlife Drive, a location managed by Blackwater National Wildlife Refuge.

Photo by Perri Meldon, 2022.

land amounting to approximately one thousand acres.[5] During the long, hard hours spent in one another's company, they formed a lifelong bond. Only after seeking permission from their respective owners did they marry, as enslaved people did not have license to wed without the consent of those who legally, though immorally, controlled their lives.

This bay, which had been forged by a meteor strike nearly 35 million years ago, was the place where the couple began to bring their own babies into the world—sons and daughters, nine in all, beautiful beacons of life.[6] But Rit and Ben did not have custody of these children. According to Maryland statute, as was typical across the slaveholding South, a child inherited the status of their mother. And Rit was unfree. Through a complicated chain of events that had transpired over time—a white woman's widowhood, her remarriage, and later her son's inheritance—Rit Green Ross was property of Edward Brodess, the young son of Mary Pattison Brodess Thompson and her first husband, and so, too, were her children. The offspring of Rit and Ben therefore belonged to their mother's legal enslavers—the Pattison-Brodesses. And after Mary Brodess Thompson's premature death, the children would be managed by Anthony Thompson, her widower, until the young Brodess came of age.

The Green-Ross family, like so many other African American families, was born into the genealogical breach that Modesty's forced exile from Africa had wrought. Members of their bloodline and loveline would always struggle with loss and heartache. Before Minty Ross crested in her mother's waters and pushed through the womb to glimpse the shadowed light of this world, she had probably already lost kin to the demon. On the Pattison plantation from which her mother hailed, enslaved girls, likely extended family members, had been sold. Minty would never know them, but she may have heard stories and feared future recurrences of familial division. While Ben and Rit had at first resided on the Thompson estate and started a family there, they would be

Harriet Tubman's locations in Dorchester County, Maryland,
circa 1800–1860.

Courtesy of Bill Nelson of Bill Nelson Maps and Kate Larson.

separated around the year 1827–28 by Rit's legal owner. After relocating Rit and the children to his farm, Edward Brodess pursued various leasing arrangements and work assignments, sending Rit to reside off-site to labor for different "employers." As soon as the couple's children became old enough, or able to work at any task that would either secure their room and board or pay dividends to their legal owners, they were also sent away. Rit and Ben had no say in these decisions as family members were placed in an unpredictable chain of serial removes to other places in the area. Their shared family life was marred by constant disorientation and painful goodbyes.

Minty had been born a middle child in a period when the practice of slavery was changing in the Upper South state of Maryland due to the expansion of cotton agriculture to the west. Around the time of the American Revolution in the 1770s and 1780s, when fertile soils had been exhausted and the tobacco economy had faltered, slaveholders in the Chesapeake began looking to other financial opportunities. They turned first to the production of grain and later to the commodification of human laborers. By the nineteenth century, cotton production was extending farther south and west into the rich lands of Native American nations that would be seized by the United States in the "Indian Removal" era of the 1820s and 1830s. White opportunists and agriculturalists migrating into these newly opened lands sought to enlarge their labor forces. For slaveholders in the Upper South, unfree Black people represented easy earnings in this changing economic environment. Maryland farmers began taking advantage of the wealth stored in the bodies of their legal slaves. Some sold individuals into cotton country, separating families; many hired out African Americans to others, who could use their labor on a temporary basis. Slaveholders also diversified their economic operations, developing flourishing timber and canal construction industries that forcibly exploited unfree people for the worst jobs while also employing free Black workers. The owners of Minty's family adopted all these financial strategies. As the shape of chattel bondage shifted in Maryland, so did the population distribution. The percentage of free African Americans increased through manumission as well as escapes as individuals relocated to the large port city of Baltimore and as higher numbers of enslaved people were leased to work beyond their legal owners' estates.[7]

Fear must have been an overriding emotion for Rit Green as she went about her daily labors in the late 1820s, caring for her own children as well as she could, keeping house for the family that possessed her, tending their children as commanded, and striving to maintain the inner strength that would enable her to rise the next morning. She could be sent away from her little ones at any time. Her children could be plucked from the physically barren but emotion-filled space of her one-room cabin. Minty Ross must have sensed, as she passed through toddlerhood, that her family was perennially poised on a dangerous precipice. At any moment, the family structure could come crashing down, breaking bonds and shattering the lives of parents and children alike. The demon Slavery had come for her kin before Minty first drew breath, and he had not relented.

Despite the odds against it in this context of trepidation and separation, Minty Ross knew familial love and care, so much so that one of her earliest memories was of parental tenderness in the material form of a wooden cradle. "In the eastern shore of Maryland Dorchester County is where I was born," a mature Harriet Tubman told Emma Telford, the white neighbor who wrote down the autobiographical testimony around the year 1905. "The first thing I remember, was lying in [the] cradle. You seen these trees that are hollow. Take a big tree, cut it down, put a bode [board] in each end, make a cradle of it and call it a 'gum. I remember lying in that there."[8] Tubman's early memory was sensory. She recalled the sensation of her small, immeasurably fragile body pressing against the flesh of the felled tree. She may have associated this physical feeling with safety and shelter, much as she would experience the touch of a tree against her back during a snowstorm decades later. Tubman does not say so in her reminiscences, but this cradle was probably carved by her father, Ben, a skilled timberman and wood-worker.

Like her father, Harriet Tubman would spend substantial time among trees during her youth. Her familiarity with the woods shows as she pauses in this recollection to specify the kind of tree that formed her cradle, as well as the method of making it. The steps she succinctly recounts in this passage would have been laborious. An unfree father like Ben had to make time for his family beyond his forced work hours for the enslaving family, carving out minutes just as he would coax forms from trees. He had to select a large tree of the correct species for the cradle—the versatile, aromatic sweet gum—then chop it down, smooth it out, and anchor it to end boards. The sweet gum was a deciduous tree common, but not predominant, in clearings and aged fields near the Chesapeake Bay. Standing on tall, grayish trunks typically ranging in size from 60 to 100 feet, sweet gums emitted a lemony mint aroma and dangled leaves shaped like stars. After their annual spring flowering, the trees dropped fruits with long stalks attached to brown balls covered by prickly points. Residents along the bay used this tree for numerous purposes. Indigenous people, who had lived in the area long before the arrival of English settlers, used the inner bark to treat ailments like diarrhea, flux, and dysentery in people as well as distemper in dogs.[9] English colonists, relative newcomers to the region since the early 1600s, scraped resin from inside the bark to chew as gum and to treat illness. And it would seem from the evidence of Minty's cradle that African Americans used the sweet gum's hardwood to craft family furnishings. Overall, lumber was the principle use for this tree, which woodworkers transformed into all manner of containers and cabinets.

Surely the crafting of one of these sweet gums into a swaying crib that would hold and rock baby Minty was a labor of love. But perhaps this wooden cradle in which Minty lay as an infant would be remembered so clearly by the mature Harriet Tubman not just because it felt safe but also because it was the last space of bodily safety and emotional security that she would ever know from childhood through young adulthood. An enslaved child was afforded only a brief stint of innocence, starting from birth and ending with that devastating moment when, as a result of some observation, or more often a death or separation, the child could perceive who—and what—society said they were: chattel, property, slaves of others who deserved the dregs of life. Soon after this cradle memory, golden-hued, like a sunset, Tubman's recollections turn dark and disordered.

As an older woman, Harriet Tubman narrated events

from her early life to biographers, supporters, and advocates and activists of the Underground Railroad network without a clear chronology, allowing the most striking, and often traumatic, occurrences to push forward in her accounts. For reasons that only she knew—perhaps the pain of remembered trauma, perhaps the prioritization of certain stories for select audiences in order to raise funds to continue her vital rescue work—Tubman did not always specify where she and her family lived when, and whether she resided on the plantation of her mother's enslaver's second husband, or on the grounds of someone who leased her, or on the land of her original enslavers' son as significant events occurred. What emerges as the clearest pattern from Tubman's early childhood remembrances is deprivation of parental presence due either to Rit's and Ben's labor-driven absence on the same grounds or to Minty's and Rit's forced relocations.

In this environment of absence, upheaval, and lack, Minty was left to her own devices at a young age. Her father was an agricultural, timber, and shipping laborer on the plantation of Anthony Thompson, where members of the Green-Ross family lived until the mid or late 1820s. Her mother was put to work in the "big house" of the Thompsons (then likely in the home of the Brodesses when her young legal owner came of age). As much as they loved Minty and longed to tend to her, Ben and Rit were forbidden this right as long as their time belonged to others. "I grew up like a neglected weed," a mature Tubman told a journalist in the 1850s, "ignorant of liberty, having no experience of it." But as Tubman knew from observation as a child made to work outdoors, and from keeping her own farm and homestead after resettling in the North in her forties, weeds were the hardiest type of plants.[10]

Minty's early childhood years were riddled with neglect. Before she reached the age of five, for hour upon hour, she had no one to watch her, soothe her, or teach her. She went about barely clothed and with her thick hair uncombed. As a four-year-old, Minty was often left "lying in that yard" while her mother "mucked" in the "big house." And these same years were also tinted by Minty's forced acclimation to a labor regimen far beyond her maturity level. Because her mother had to leave her own small children to cook for the family of their enslavers, Minty was tasked with caring for her younger siblings and infant brother—probably Ben, Rachel, and Henry.[11] A small child herself, eager to play and romp and pretend, she treated her baby brother like a rag doll. Though age appropriate, this behavior was alarming, as Minty pretended the baby was a "pig in a bag" and held him upside down by the bottom of his "dress." Tubman remembered being so small when she swung the baby that his head and arms would brush against the cabin floor. She also recalled her feeling of anticipation before her mother would set out for the big house each day, leaving her on her own to explore and experiment.

Already at around four years old, Minty showed clear signs of willfulness. She relished being in charge of herself and having endless time to "play." But she was so young and ill-equipped to care for a baby that she could have accidentally harmed her brother. Her mother worked in the big house "late nights," leaving the infant to fuss and cry with only Minty to tend his needs. Minty would try to stop her brother's high-pitched wails by "cut[ting] a fat chunk of pork and toast[ing] it on the coals and put[ting] it in his mouth." One night, when her mother returned and saw the baby's lips stuffed with charred meat, she thought Minty had "done kill him." Rit must have been terrified, racked with guilt, and even angry with her daughter in that moment, imagining that she had lost a son to the conditions that forced her to leave one young child in the care of another. After correcting Harriet, Rit must have laid her tired bones down on the "board box" and "straw" that served as her bed, relieved that her babies still breathed, awakening the next day in a tangle of sweet children's limbs to renew the exhausting cycle of work and fear.[12]

Minty "nursed that baby till he was so big [she] couldn't tote him any more," which means her little brother grew to toddlerhood without the regular presence of a mother.[13] Once her brother had outgrown her capacity to carry him, Minty seems to have had even more leeway while left alone during the day to explore Rit's cabin or the plantation out-buildings. Perhaps it was during these unsupervised hours when she could range across the yard that Minty first began to notice the properties of weeds—the outcast but robust type of plant to which she would later compare herself. She had already shown a sense of adventure when left alone with the baby, and with relatively free unchaperoned time that was the result of adult neglect, she applied her creativity in ways that involved riskier experiments.

When she got "mischievous about the house," at around the age of six, Minty's nightmare of being snatched away came true. Edward Brodess, the son of Mary Pattison Brodess Thompson and her first husband, took charge of Rit's family. He relocated them from the Thompson estate to his late father's farm, then removed Minty from her mother's cabin and sent Minty "out to learn to be a weaver." Minty was so poorly provided for that she "hadn't any clothes" when she was first sent away to work. Her mistress-enslaver, Edward Brodess's wife, Eliza Ann, made her a "petticoat" for the occasion, perhaps to save face at so poorly clothing the people her spouse owned. On the day that Minty was to leave her mother for the first time, she watched "a man come after

[her] riding horseback." He seated her on the horse "in front of him" and carried her off into the void.

The Brodesses leased Minty out because she was more trouble to them than they thought she was worth. Young children of enslaved parents could be a financial burden on their enslavers, requiring, as they did, even a minimal amount of care and feeding. By placing Minty with another white family who could use her labor, her owners could save the expense of feeding and clothing her while having her trained in desirable skills. The Brodesses wanted pesky Minty sent off-site for the time being and expected a tamed child who could spin thread to be returned in her place. Around this time, in the mid-1820s into the 1840s, Edward Brodess also sold Rit's older daughters, Mariah Ritty, Linah, and Soph, turning, as the historian Kate Clifford Larson has written, "slaves into cash." Rit's already fractured heart would have splintered all the more at the temporary loss of her willful Araminta.[14]

On the new farm three miles away, where the man on horseback deposited Minty, everything was frightening and foreign to her. She had no mother to turn to at night and no siblings to squeeze and tease. She had never spent significant time inside white people's homes, and she feared their nearness. Merely watching them eat at the supper table paralyzed her. How did she feel standing before people like those who commanded her own parents and demeaned those who shared her brown skin? Wrong, bad, dirty, ugly? She didn't know what to do with her body or where to direct her eyes. Shame is among the harshest and most debilitating emotions a person can feel, and it was the word a mature Harriet Tubman would use to describe her memory of that childhood experience in the home of her new "masters." As a girl not yet big enough to reach a dining room sideboard, she had been too "ashamed to stand up and eat before them."[15]

Minty must have been hungry, thirsty, and long deprived of fresh foods, but she refused to drink the "sweet milk" offered to her by the mistress of this household and stood as still as possible at the edge of the dining room. But even this paralysis in a new and hazardous situation revealed a strength in Minty's young character. At just six years old, she was dignified and self-disciplined. Despite a sense of shame at her physical body (the space she occupied, her outward appearance, and her biological needs) and her fear of the terrifying unknown (what might happen if she ate white people's food in front of them), Minty exhibited a stubborn pride. She would not take a beverage offered from this table, no matter how tempting it might be. "I stuck to it, that I didn't drink sweet milk," she later said.[16] It seems that Minty had decided not to further expose herself before these dangerous strangers by revealing her wants or risking a misstep, even if that kind of backbone resulted in further deprivation. Before the age of ten, then, Minty had the ability to defer gratification in service of her intention to pursue greater ends, in this case, self-protection.

Minty wrestled with fear and pride, shame and loneliness, when she was too young to make sense of this barrage of mainly negative feelings. She was gutted by heartache and lived each day in extreme emotional isolation. Desperate for her mother, Minty longed to be back home in Rit's cabin, so much so that she imagined Rit had a real bed that she might crawl into. Later, Tubman would express that rare was the poor child who had been as homesick as she was during that time of initial separation. "I used to sleep on the floor in front of the fireplace and there I'd lie and cry and cry. I used to think all the time if I could only get home and get in my mother's bed, and the funny part of that was, she never had a bed in her life. Nothing but a board box nailed up against the wall and straw laid on it."[17]

Minty feared eating in front of others and slept on the bare floor. And these were the times in her day when she was at relative ease, not being forced to work at tasks far above her maturity level. The couple who now had charge of her, James Cook and his wife (unnamed in the record), expected outrageous output from this small, lonely child. Mrs. Cook, a weaver, set about teaching Minty the skills of spinning thread from natural fibers and weaving thread into cloth, which required focused attention, hand-eye-foot coordination, and practiced dexterity. When Minty resisted this tedious work that kept her cramped within stuffy rooms, the Cooks reassigned her to gruesome outside labor. James Cook was, among other things, a trapper who dealt in musk-rat hides, a profitable business, given the desirability of the animals' pelts. When the weather turned cool, Cook set his traps along streams and marshes where salt water from the bay intermixed with inland tributaries. He then sent out Minty, who was around age six, to collect the dead animals once their bodies had been broken by his iron traps. To gather the carcasses of these animals in wintertime when the pelts were at their thickest, Minty had to wade in the chilly water with no shoes or protective clothing. Uncomfortably submerged to her ankles or calves, she had to free the lifeless creatures from their sharp and rusty traps, risking injury to her hands and perhaps thinking of how she, too, was a small, snared mammal.[18]

When Minty fell ill from collecting dead muskrats in the damp and the mud, she was put to work at the spinning wheel indoors again. "Another attempt was made to teach her weaving," wrote Tubman's first biographer, Sarah Bradford, "but she would not learn, for she hated her mistress, and did not want to live at home, as she would have done as a weaver, for it was the custom then to weave the cloth for the family, or a part of it, in the house."[19] Minty had been headstrong when it came to drinking the Cooks' sweet milk, and she showed that same strength of character when she refused to learn how to weave their cloth.

As a child who had no choice about where she was sent and what she would be assigned to do there, Minty learned the power of refusal. The Cooks could make her carry out rote physical actions, but they did not control her mind. They were not privy to Minty's thoughts, so they may have assumed she was too dumb or clumsy to be tutored. This was a grave error in judgment that many people who owned, leased, or sought to control this headstrong girl would repeat. They believed she could not do things, when in fact she *would* not, or simply *had* not . . . yet. Minty, it seems, was a child who watched and waited, suffering harsh work routines even as she learned her own mind and how to direct her willpower in order to act with conviction when she determined it counted the most.

Minty lived with this couple for two years, her young body wearing down from environmental hazards and overwork. When she contracted the measles while extracting limp muskrat bodies from metal traps, the dissatisfied renters of human children sent her home. Back in Rit's cabin and under her mother's ministrations, Minty slowly regained her health. When she was well enough to work, the Brodesses leased her out again.[20] Rit would have no input, of course, on these plans for her girl-child of fragile health.

At the age of around seven, Minty was sent to the home of a woman who wanted to pay cheap rates for a chattel-child to clean house and care for her own infant. So Minty was plucked from her mother's cabin and "put into the wagon without a word of explanation and driven off to the lady's house."[21] Once there, Minty would learn, like other enslaved children, that the teaching tools of slavery's classroom were the whip, or stick, or rod. Elizabeth Keckley, who was originally enslaved in Virginia and would eventually buy her freedom through the proceeds of her exquisite dressmaking and then write a memoir, remembered being sent to the big house to tend her mistress's infant as a four-year-old. Assigned to rock the cradle and keep the flies away from the baby, Elizabeth rocked too vigorously, tumbled the baby to the floor, and tried to scoop it up with a fireplace implement because she knew no better. Keckley was punished with a severe "lashing," learning the hard way how *not* to babysit. Domestic education would be similarly treacherous for Minty in Maryland.[22] She had never been taught how to properly care for an infant, or how to dust and polish a house like the one in which she now worked. Nevertheless, Susan, the woman who had leased her, expected perfection. When Minty failed at "sweeping and dusting a parlor" to the standards of this temporary mistress, stirring up dust that resettled on the furniture, "reproaches, and savage words, fell upon the ears of the frightened child, and she was commanded to do the work all over again," Bradford recounted.[23]

Cleaning was Minty's secondary job in this home. Her primary assignment was minding the infant. "I was only seven years old when I was sent away to take car[e] of a baby," an elderly Tubman remembered. "I was so little that I had to sit down on the floor and he[ave] the baby to put it in my lap. And that baby was always in my lap [ex]cept when it was asleep, or its mother was feeding it."[24] After babysitting and cleaning all day with a whip in plain sight as an unsubtle threat, Minty was expected to provide childcare throughout the night. If she fell asleep while rocking Susan's baby, she was awakened by a whipping. Susan, a mean woman encouraged in her sadism by culture and law, slept with the rawhide device under her pillow.[25] And Minty's own sweet cradle, shaped from the perfumed gum tree, was by then a distant memory.

Seven years old. The treatment that Minty suffered, the cold, cruel disregard, is still heartbreaking to contemplate two hundred years after the fact. Her testimony, and that of other captive children, compels us to dwell with the grave assault that slavery was on childhood as a phase of life as well as on young spirits. But even as Minty faced the blows and recriminations of grown white people, she was learning how to thwart them with the sheer force of her developing determination. Araminta "Minty" Green-Ross was as fresh and sharp as her name would indicate. She would continue in the mode that she had inaugurated at the Cooks, refusing to be forced into total compliance.

Food was again the battlefield where Minty resisted the will of those who exploited her. At the Cooks' home, she had declined the sweet milk they offered as if they thought this meager gesture could compensate for child abuse. But in Susan's house, she had grown bold enough in white people's presence to sneak a delicacy. Minty would not be the first enslaved child to crave sweetness in the midst of dietary austerity, but she seems to have indulged that desire only on her own terms. Minty, much like abused children in our own time, was keenly aware of the moods and behaviors of the adults in charge of her. This was a coping strategy, a defensive posture used to aid in the anticipation of increased threat. On a day when she noticed Susan arguing with her husband, Minty took advantage of Susan's distraction to sneak a bit of sugar. Telling the story in her own words, a mature Tubman said: "After breakfast she had the baby, and I stood by the table waiting till I was to take it; just by me was a bowl of lumps of white sugar . . . I never had nothing good; no sweet, no sugar, an[d] that sugar, right by me, did look so nice, and my Missus's back turned to me while she was fighting with her husband, so I just put my fingers in the sugar bowl to take one lump."[26] But Susan noticed and reached for her omnipresent whip with her husband by her side. Divided just moments before by a heated interpersonal conflict, the defiance of a slave child brought the couple back into sync.

Instead of acquiescing to another beating, Minty fled. She crossed the threshold with the outraged pair chasing behind her and plunged outdoors into the open. "I just flew, and they didn't catch me." She ran across spongy fields and past isolated homes until she wore herself out, then came upon "a great pig-pen." Because she was "too little to climb into it," Tubman recalled, she "tumbled into the high board, and fell in on the ground." From Friday to Tuesday, Minty lived with "eight or ten little pigs" and their mother, "fighting with those little pigs for the potato peelings and other scraps that came down the trough." Desperately hungry and fearful that the "ole sow" might hurt her for taking the piglets' food, Minty gave up the temporary haven she had found with the animals. Dirty, exhausted, and "starved," she returned to the abusive household of her temporary owners and was promptly beaten by Susan's husband, an assault that left lifelong scars. After three months in Susan's prison-house, Minty was "again returned to her mother . . . worn to skin and bone and with her neck disfigured with a great scare [sic]," recounted Emma Telford.[27] Minty paid dearly for her recalcitrance, but she also learned that she could run, that she could withstand extreme circumstances, and that she could abide, at least for a time, in the semiwild with nonhuman animals.

Did Minty pray during those days that she curled up in the pigpen? Most likely, yes, as she already had a religious sense as a young child. An older Harriet Tubman would recall, as recorded and summarized by an acquaintance, Ednah Dow Cheney, an ironically "pious mistress" (perhaps this same Susan), who physically punished her routinely, for "every slight or fancied fault." When Minty recognized this pattern, she "prepared for it by putting on all the thick clothes she could procure to protect her skin." And it is in the description of a sartorial self-defense strategy that Minty's own spiritual life glints in the background. "When invited into family prayers, she preferred to stay on the landing, and pray for herself," Cheney wrote, then quoted Tubman: "'And I prayed to God . . . to make me strong and able to fight, and that's what I've always prayed for ever since.'" Cheney, to whom Tubman told this story, indicates that she tried to "persuade" Tubman that this sort of prayer was "wrong."

But Tubman rejected Cheney's interpretation, insisting the prayer was not only "right" but also "sincere."[28]

As a young child, Minty Ross was developing her own practice for communicating with the God of her burgeoning belief—through prayer in private. And more than that, she was forming her own understanding of the difference between right and wrong. Abuse of the powerless by the powerful was wrong. Defending oneself against such abuse was right. The God to whom she appealed would, she thought, positively judge her request for a fighting chance in this unjust circumstance. To Minty's mind, God justified battling against one's oppressors. But the question remained open as to whether he would equip her in that war.

2

THE STARS

My Lord, what a morning, My Lord, what a morning! My Lord, what a morning. When the stars begin to fall, when the stars begin to fall.

—"MY LORD, WHAT A MORNING,"
TRADITIONAL SPIRITUAL

The midnight sky and the silent stars
have been the witnesses of your devotion to freedom.

—FREDERICK DOUGLASS,
LETTER TO HARRIET TUBMAN, 1868

Childhood trauma led Minty Ross to seek divine inter-vention. This was an experience, and a reaction, that she shared with other unfree girls. Black women who published spiritual memoirs in the nineteenth century spoke of early separations from parents, states of captivity as slaves or servants, and appeals to the God of their belief that echoed Minty's. The girl who would become the traveling preacher known as Old Elizabeth recited a memoir that accords most closely with Harriet Tubman's early years. Born in Maryland to enslaved parents in 1766, Elizabeth told her story at age ninety-seven to an unnamed person who wrote it down (we must assume with a degree of editorial license). Elizabeth's family lived together when she was a young child, presumably on the grounds of the person who enslaved them.

Her parents were practicing Methodists. Her father was literate and read the Bible aloud to his family each Sunday morning. "When I was but five years old, I often felt the overshadowing of the Lord's Spirit," Elizabeth narrated, "and these incomes and influences co[n]tinued to attend me until I was eleven years old." But Elizabeth's domestic stability cratered when, like Minty, Elizabeth was leased out by the man who owned her family. At the age of eleven, Elizabeth was taken. "My master sent me to another farm, several miles from my parents, brothers, and sisters which was a great trouble to me. At last I grew so lonely and sad I thought I should die, if I did not see my mother," she later wrote. Desolate, Elizabeth escaped to find her mother, wandering twenty miles before she was successful. She remained with her mother for several days until she was sent back to her new placement of bondage, which "renewed [her] sorrows." Elizabeth's mother had one parting gift for her child, the stark advice that Elizabeth had "'nobody in the wide world to look to but God.'" Elizabeth repeated these words to herself like a mantra—"none but God in the wide world"—as she trod back to the farm where the overseer stood waiting to tie her up and beat her. Elizabeth remembered her mother's words, clung to them like a lifeboat, and tried to look to God over the following difficult weeks and months. "I betook myself to prayer, and in every lonely place I found an altar. I mourned sore like a dove and chattered forth my sorrow, moaning in the corners of the field, and under the fences."[1] She seemed to feel that God alone could understand her pain, bearing out the truth of her mother's adage.

Minty and Elizabeth were not alone in their desperate appeal to an unseen presence for emotional comfort in the wake of familial separation and physical abuse. Zilpha Elaw, who would preach in private homes in the States and then abroad in London in the 1840s, also turned to God to ease her childhood sufferings. Zilpha was born free in Pennsylvania to "religious parents" around the year 1790. She was then orphaned as a child and sent to live and work as a servant in a white Quaker household. Zilpha felt lonely in this new home, especially in the absence of familiar Methodist religious rituals observed by her deceased parents. Punctuating this pall of loneliness were her mistress's "very severe rebukes." A desolate Zilpha turned to God in her troubles. "How vast a source of consolation did I derive from habitual communion with my God; to Him I repaired in secret to acquaint him with all my griefs, and obtained both sympathy and succor," she attested.[2] Her sense of a divine and compassionate listener, introduced by her then absent parents, eased her suffering.

Minty Ross likewise took an early religious education with her when she was sent by her enslavers to labor on distant estates as a child. Her mother, Rit, and father, Ben, were practicing Christians. Bazzel's Church, a small Methodist Episcopal denomination in Dorchester County surrounded by marshy ground and forest, was remembered by local residents as a place where Tubman's family sometimes worshipped.[3] Ben fasted on Fridays as an act of religious devotion. His practice suggests a Catholic or Episcopalian influence, though Tubman told her biographer, Bradford, that he did it for conscience rather than for denominational adherence.[4] As an adult, Tubman would continue this dietary observance. Ben may also have held non-Christian beliefs espoused by other Black enslaved people who revered ancestral spirits and made protective talismans out of natural elements like roots. The informal institution of the pre-emancipation Black church drew on "West African religious concepts . . . blending them syncretistically with orthodox colonial Christianity," explained the theologian Katie Geneva Cannon.[5] Oral historical and archaeological evidence supports this picture of enslaved people embracing a Christian faith enhanced by West African influences and practices. A white man whose great-grandfather bought Anthony Thompson's land, where Tubman's family had once been enslaved, remembered that his grandfather believed in witches and sought a remedy for dispelling one from a local Black woman.[6] The Maryland state-sponsored archaeological study conducted at a cabin that may have once served as a slave quarters on Thompson's land uncovered an unusual assemblage of objects currently interpreted as a "spirit cache." The collection of special items, including "a glass heart-shaped perfume bottle stopper, a white ceramic dish, and a copper alloy button," might have been positioned near the fireplace to ward off evil spirits.[7] The religious faith of Minty and her family, like that of other local residents, was most likely

Bazzel's Church, Dorchester County, Maryland. Notice the forested landscape and water channel that still remain.

Photo by Perri Meldon, 2023.

richly variegated, lending Minty access to various channels of fortitude, relief, and appeal as she was shuttled about from farm to farm.

According to Sarah Bradford, the mature Harriet Tubman claimed to "always know when there [was] danger near her" and said this gift of foresight had been "inherited" from her father, who accurately predicted the weather as well as future events such as the U.S. war with Mexico in 1846. If Ben Ross was Catholic, he may have been even more inclined to combine African-derived faith practices with Christian beliefs, an approach commonly associated with enslaved people in the Caribbean and Brazil who adapted the Catholicism of their Spanish, French, and Portuguese enslavers. Rit Green and Ben Ross were religious people who instilled in their children a sense of a spiritual reality beyond the mundane, visible world. "I have known many of her family," Sarah Bradford said of Tubman; "they all seem to be peculiarly intelligent, upright and religious people, and to have a strong feeling of family affection." Acknowledging Bradford's bias here in labeling a smart Black family as "peculiar," we can still gather from this observation a sense of the family's moral grounding and religious devotion. The Green-Rosses, along with fellow enslaved families across the Eastern Shore of Maryland's Chesapeake Bay, participated in cultures of integrated belief, story, and ritual.[8]

Minty would have navigated this rich and diverse local religious landscape, which included freely chosen as well as mandatory elements. Noting that Rit's owner required attendance at Methodist services, the contemporary Tubman biographer and historian Kate Larson has commented: "Tubman and her family likely integrated a number of religious practices and ideas into their daily lives."[9] This vibrant religious environment was enhanced by the context of the Second Great Awakening in the early nineteenth century, a fervent Protestant movement of revival and reform sweeping across the nation. Minty had been exposed to this complex mixture of multidenominational Christianity and African heritage folk beliefs as a young child. Even during the long periods of exile from home, she was sent back to her mother when illness struck, steeping her once again in her familiar faith surrounds and affording her time to gather spiritual and emotional reinforcements.

And while she was working, praying, pining, and sporadically seeing her mother, Minty was interpreting the charged social relations around her. What did she learn from these childhood scenes? Certainly, she understood the power of the color line to differentiate black from white, enslaved from free, and abusers from abused. And she found that carving out notches of autonomy during her daily trials— small spaces within which to do what she wanted or to refuse what she did not want—was necessary to her developing identity and intrinsic dignity. During her trying time with the swine in the stall, she may have compared her lot to that of the hungry piglets. She might have compared her mother's straw "bed" to the sow's, too, and considered how her family, like the porcine family, spent their hard lives corralled in places mandated by those of a certain race and status. She had observed from a young age that some people had a mysterious right to command and separate her family. And sometime during her youth, she had witnessed a devastating event: two sisters sold and "carried away" on a chain gang.[10]

Following this tragedy, Minty "saw the hopeless grief of the poor old mother, and the silent despair of the aged father, and already she began to revolve in her mind the question "'Why should such things be?'" This last line, presented in quotation marks by Sarah Bradford, captured the young Minty's burning question. She wanted to know why some families were made to suffer at the hands of others. And she followed up this pointed interrogative about social inequality and caste sadism with a second question, and perhaps appeal, that Bradford quotes directly. "'Is there no deliverance for my people?'"[11]

These existential questions emerged from Minty's specific circumstances as an enslaved girl growing up on the

Chesapeake Bay, a singular place that a meteor made, but they were also expressions of universal matters that go to the heart of the human experience on any earthly landscape. In her ranging philosophical and scientific study about the mystery of life, the cell biologist Ursula Goodenough has suggested that there is a singular pair of questions "fundamental to human concern." These queries probe "How Things Are and Which Things Matter." The first question, Goodenough says, is an inquiry into cosmology, while the second is an exploration of morality. All major religions of the world address both ulterior questions, writes Goodenough, which is why these faiths have attracted devoted adherents across millennia.[12] Steeped in a teeming religious surround, the young and astute Minty Ross seems to have been poking a stick into this same philosophical thicket. Minty's first question—"Why should such things be?"—probed the rationale for slavery, functioning as a cosmological inquiry into the genesis and development of human relations of bondage. "Would there be deliverance?," her second question, asked whether the infraction of slavery was significant enough, and whether her people were precious enough, for God to take action. Here she was testing the contours and logics of morality—what counts as good, what counts as bad, and who counts as worthy. While scholars and sages still strive to address the first of Minty's questions, in the worldview of her enslaved Christian community, only God could answer the second. And in her later childhood years while her family was still being splintered, Minty may have felt that God was keeping silent.

Elizabeth, Jarena Lee, Zilpha Elaw, and Julia Foote, who would all become "holy" women during Harriet Tubman's lifetime, also struggled during their youths to find clarity, certainty, and consistency in their relationship with God. Their difficult experiences offer guidance for understanding Minty's formative years that are mostly obscured in the historical record. Julia Foote, for example, was born free in New York to formerly enslaved parents whose freedom had been bought through her father's exhaustive excess labors. Julia was eight years old when she experienced a religious "conversion" as a minister from her parents' church prayed with her at home. Eager to learn how to read the Bible, she begged her father to teach her. He knew just enough to guide her through learning the alphabet, which she paired with reciting the Lord's prayer during her regular devotions. But when she turned ten, Julia experienced a cleavage from family common to all these women's memories. For reasons that she did not state, but likely were economic, her parents sent her away to serve as a domestic in the home of a family in the countryside. There, Julia found decent treatment and a place to pray in the barn. But when she was told to bring "some little pound cakes" up from the cellar, she learned that her mistress's kindly attitude had limits. The woman accused Julia of eating cakes in secret, which the child denied. Julia later wrote: "[She] frightened me so by her looks and action that I trembled so violently I could not speak." The mistress whipped Julia until the point of fatigue and threatened to repeat the punishment the next day. Julia ran away to her mother, who sent her back. This trial tested Julia's faith, and her prayers faded as she felt that God may have abandoned her.[13]

The years of Minty's preadolescence and early teens brought tumult and trouble to the Green-Ross family and may have caused her to doubt God's nearness as Julia had. The sale of Minty's sisters, which likely occurred in the mid-1820s to mid-1840s, was the most memorable and painful occurrence in her young life. Minty herself may have been marked for potential sale in this period along with her siblings. She later experienced visions and nightmares repeating the horrible scene on a loop—of women and children snatched away from all that they knew. "She never closed her eyes," Bradford related, "that she did not imagine she saw horsemen coming, and heard the screams of women and children, as they were being dragged away to far worse slavery than that they were enduring there."[14] These sororal sales, which must have felt like deaths in the family, may have led to a crisis of faith for Minty. And in addition to losing three older sisters to their owner's financial roulette, including two sales that she witnessed, Minty nearly lost her youngest brother, Moses. Around the early 1840s, Edward Brodess brokered a sale of little Moses and lied to Rit Green, the woman who had nursed, bathed, and fed him as a child. Edward told Rit he was merely sending the boy on a short errand. But Rit had observed this man and his family for decades, and she sensed the subterfuge regarding her son. She grabbed Moses and ran away to the woody damp of what was most likely Greenbriar Swamp, hiding her child in the wilderness for a month.[15] Rit was a religious woman. She must have made a church of those woods during the weeks that she lay in wait, trying to force Edward Brodess's hand. Perhaps the God of her belief answered her prayers. For she won this battle. Brodess revoked the sale. Rit and Moses returned. And Minty saw in her mother a model of that same fierce bravery, that same willingness to run and find shelter in nature, that she herself had demonstrated at age seven and would exhibit time and again as an adult.

There were tragedies, and there were miracles during Minty's childhood in chattel slavery. During one of those frequent periods when she was working far from home, she escaped at night, as had become her custom, to visit her mother. It was late autumn, the time for oak leaves to flash gold before their descent, when Minty ducked into the cabin under the cover of darkness. At eleven years old, Minty had learned that for the unfree, night provided a tasseled curtain of secrecy. While she visited with her mother, perhaps sharing a chunk of corn bread, or sewing lines on a hand-pieced quilt, or trading stories and information about community goings-on, one of her brothers stood guard outside. At any moment, a white patroller assigned to watch for slaves without passes could spot her, snatch her, and have her returned and punished. Minty must have been startled, and Rit, too, when the boy called suddenly from outside the cabin. Gesturing wildly at the door, he urged Minty to "come out and see the stars!" Minty slipped out of the rude dwelling and found that the darkness was no longer solid. A spray of lights pierced the night and rained down to earth. With her brother beside her, Minty saw the stars "all shooting whichway," a moment she would remember forever after. Scores of other enslaved people across the South saw this celestial pageant, too, remembering the event as the night the stars "fell" or "showered down and disappeared" like "sparkles."[16]

Minty, her brother, and people of all races and statuses across the country were witnessing an astounding astrological

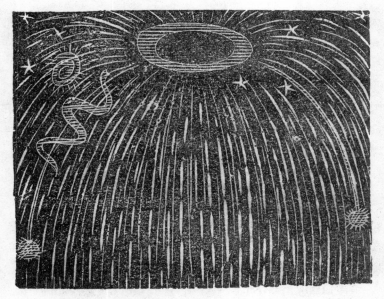

This drawing of the Leonid meteor shower was made soon after the event and appeared in *Mechanics' Magazine*, November 1833.

Public domain.

phenomenon now known as the 1833 Leonid meteor storm. In the wee hours of the night and early morning on November 12 and 13, nearly one hundred thousand blazing "stars" plunged toward the earth like a spray of firecrackers. The deluge consisted of cast-off particles from the Tempel-Tuttle comet, giving the appearance of uncountable stars in motion. This was, as the anthropologist Candace Greene has put it, "space debris" of an unusually spectacular nature. The phenomenon was so amazing that observers represented it through a range of cultural forms, from drawing, to rhetoric, to quilting, to scientific investigation. Indigenous peoples of the Great Plains who recorded significant annual events in the pictographic chronologies known as "winter counts" painted images of the starfall on buffalo hides to such an extent that the event appears in nearly all known examples. Lakotas and other groups who created this record remembered the occurrence as "The Year the Stars Fell" or "The Storm of Stars." Throughout the country, many of those who witnessed the star shower saw an invisible hand at work. Churchgoers in the South, North, and West attributed the event to the hand of God. Scholars, in contrast, saw natural forces at play and developed the study of meteor science based on their hypotheses.[17] Experience of the event was preserved in the African American oral tradition, through the stories of formerly enslaved people, and perhaps the spiritual later sung by the great American contralto Marian Anderson: "My Lord, what a morning... when the stars begin to fall." In Georgia, the expert quilter Harriet Powers was not yet born when the meteor burst, but she would later hear of the event and represent it through cloth on a quilt. "The falling of the stars on November 13, 1833," Harriet Powers's description of this quilt square began. "The people were frighten and thought that the end of time had come God's hand staid the stars. The varmints rushed out of their beds,"

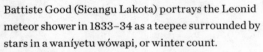

Battiste Good (Sicangu Lakota) portrays the Leonid meteor shower in 1833–34 as a teepee surrounded by stars in a waníyetu wówapi, or winter count.

Image reproduced with permission from the National Anthropological Archives, Smithsonian Institution.

Harriet Powers's pictorial quilt square of the Leonid meteor shower depicts human and nonhuman life among the falling stars.

Photograph © Fall 2024 Museum of Fine Arts, Boston. Image reproduced with permission from MFA, Boston.

her commentary continued.[18] Harriet Powers related the story as told to her, orally recounting the scene she had sewn onto her quilt square as a religious occurrence. The sky had seemed to be falling, but God had caught it, rescuing his creation before it was too late.

Like Harriet Powers, who had grown up enslaved in the late 1830s and 1840s, Minty Ross interpreted the falling stars as apocalyptic. In the seconds and minutes that she stared into a transformed nightscape that November, Minty thought "the end of the world had come."[19] She shared this view with other enslaved people who witnessed the flying stars that night, observed white masters and overseers running outside in awe and fear, and thought it could be Judgment Day—the ultimate moment of reckoning when God would punish the guilty, including enslavers of human beings. Although the sky settled down after the last star fell and slaveholders still held sway when dawn finally rose, some unfree people may have felt that through this strange event God had signaled his presence and shown his hand. As she traveled back from her mother's cabin to her place of work before daybreak, contemplating a God who slingshot the stars like marbles, perhaps Minty inferred a reply to her second universal question after years of wondering if God was listening. Was there any deliverance for her people? Could the system of slavery ever be brought down? Maybe if the sky could fall at the hands of God, slavery could, too. Whatever conclusions she drew that night, Minty Ross had been touched by stardust, and she would forever after shine.

Nearly two years after she witnessed this celestial spectacle, Minty experienced another life-changing event. She was around twelve or thirteen years old and had been hired out as a field hand, this time to a man in the county whom she remembered as the worst in the neighborhood.[20] The exact date of this incident is not recorded, and details of the encounter differ in the accounts of Tubman's nineteenth-century confidantes. Indeed, the story of this injury as re-told takes on a mythic quality of the exceptional moment when a hero is made. We have already seen, though, that Minty's stalwart character was in formation years before this incident. And we shall soon see that her adoption of a new consciousness following this assault, more than the event itself, supercharged her spiritual life.

Like the meteor shower Minty observed, and her own escape from slavery years later, this next significant event also occurred in autumn, a season of change and preparation. The story has been told many times, in many ways. The version of the incident that hews most closely to accuracy is likely the one rendered in the elder Tubman's voice as quoted by Emma Telford. Minty was standing outside a dry goods store on a country road where she had accompanied the en-slaved cook on the new farm to procure supplies, when she saw an enslaved boy or teen run toward the village store. An overseer chased the boy into the shop, grabbed a two-pound weight from the counter used to measure goods, and hurled it at his target. As rendered in the adult Tubman's quoted narration: "One night I went out with the cook to the store to get some things for the house. I had a shoulder shawl of the mistress over my head and when I got to the store I was [a]shamed to go in and [saw] the overseer raising up his arm to throw an iron weight at one of the slaves . . . was the last I knew." Minty seems to have purposefully interceded by stepping forward to block the overseer's action. The weight intended for the "young slave" slammed into her instead, causing her to lose consciousness. "That weight struck me in the head and broke my skull and cut a piece of that shawl clean off and drove it into my head. They carried me to the home all bleeding and fainting. I had no bed, no place to lie down on at all, and they lay me on the seat of the loom, and I stayed there all that day and next, and next day I went to work again and I worked with the blood and sweat rolling down my face till I couldn't see."[21] Minty's inner and outer condition of suffering, as well as her bravery and perseverance, surface in this memory. As an adolescent girl whose life was characterized by neglect, she continued to struggle with intense feelings of shame about her bodily presentation and appearance, as indicated by her attempt to cover her unkempt hair with a shawl. She was, at the same time, so devalued by those who leased her that she had nowhere to sleep on the premises and had to return to work in the fields in an unbearable state of pain. Though happenstance, we can notice the symbolism, and indeed the irony, of Minty's broken, bleeding body crumpled upon a wooden loom, the very instrument she had resisted learning to use when she was first leased out nearly a

decade prior. Minty may have felt, in these moments immediately following the incident, that the demon Slavery still
gripped her in its infernal machinery.

Minty never fully recovered from this unexpected attack. Afterward, she would sometimes appear dazed and
confused to observers, or she would suddenly suffer periods of
unconsciousness. "The injury thus inflicted," Bradford wrote,
"causes her often to fall into a state of somnolency from
which it is almost impossible to rouse her. Disabled and sick,
her flesh all wasted away, she was returned to her owner.
He tried to sell her, but no one would buy her." Twenty-first-
century biographers of Tubman, writing in an era of more
nuanced medical knowledge, have attributed these symptoms to traumatic brain injury leading to a form of temporal
lobe epilepsy. In her own time, Minty's owner judged her, in
Tubman's later quoted words, as "not worth a sixpence" because of her resulting illness and disability.[22] He was wrong
in this assessment, of course. Minty and her young life were
priceless, even as that life would be changed by a new set of
limitations. In our time, the historian of medicine and slavery, Deirdre Cooper Owens, has argued that "we owe her the
respect to add the adjective 'disabled' to Tubman's list of descriptions when we discuss her identities."[23]

While Minty's owner tried in vain to hand her off as
damaged goods, Rit, who knew her child's true worth, nursed

Minty back to health again. Over the final weeks of fall and into winter, Minty recovered slowly through Rit's ministrations. As winter closed in around the drafty cabin, bringing with it harsh winds and introspective moods, Minty communed with God. "Already," Telford wrote of Minty's time "back [in] her old home after this occurrence . . . she had begun to ponder over the sorrows of her people . . . to see visions and 'hear the voices.'"[24]

This prolonged period of isolation—in her sickbed and in her own mind—was a critical phase in Minty's life when she may have passed into a new state of spiritual existence that Black women of her faith culture referred to as "conversion."[25] The preacher Elizabeth, for example, had been twelve years old when she had a life-altering encounter with God. Enslaved in Maryland like Minty, Elizabeth had been warned by her mother that she had no one to look to but God before she was returned to the abusive overseer who immediately beat her for having temporarily run away. Elizabeth mourned for six months, crying and feeling that her "head were waters." She stopped eating and became so weak that she could barely work. She was forced to carry out her tasks nonetheless and suffered psychologically as well as physically, to the point that she "expected to die." From within "an awful gulf of misery," she heard a voice telling her to pray. As Elizabeth obeyed the voice, she had a vision of a spiritual guide dressed in white. The guide showed her the "pit" of hell, even as she felt that she was "sustained by some invisible power." Within the frame of her terrifying vision, "the Saviour" appeared and stretched out a hand. The voice of the Lord asked her if she was "willing to be saved," and Elizabeth answered yes. She was "filled with light and . . . shown the world lying in wickedness." God then instructed her that she must "call the people to repentance." At "not yet thirteen years old," Elizabeth "felt like a new creature in Christ." Every day following this, she went into the haystacks to pray, not knowing if or when God would deliver her from slavery or how her call to preach could possibly be realized.[26]

Zilpha Elaw had been sent out to work as a domestic servant of Quakers in Pennsylvania when, at the age of fourteen, she felt "an effectual call to [her] soul." God had given her a dream of Judgment Day featuring the angel Gabriel. When she awoke, she cried, meditated, and prayed. Zilpha tried for months to believe God had forgiven her of her sins, but she could not be sure until she had a vision. Zilpha was "milking in the cow stall" and singing a hymn about seeing Jesus when she saw a "tall figure" with "long hair" and "a long white robe down to the feet" standing with "open arms" before her. To check her sight of the unusual visage, Zilpha looked to the cow she had been milking and found that the animal offered confirmation. "The beast gave forth her evidence to the reality of the heavenly appearance," Zilpha wrote, "for she turned her head and looked round as I did; and when she saw, she bowed her knees and cowered down upon the ground." Zilpha said of that miraculous moment in which she and the cow saw Jesus: "My soul was set at glorious liberty."[27]

Julia Foote, who had struggled with being accused of stealing cakes and sent back to the home where she worked as a child servant in upstate New York, returned to live with her parents years later. She was fifteen when she went to a Methodist meeting near her parents' home, heard a voice in her head, and "fell to the floor unconscious." She was carried home, then entered a trance during which she heard the voice and saw a light. The voice gave her a song, and she felt "joy and peace . . . filling her heart." She felt herself being "redeemed" and could then sing the heavenly song as a "wonderfully saved" girl.[28] Around the same time of life as Minty's accident—early adolescence—these other captive Black girls found God in a dramatic experience of religious conversion (metamorphosis into a new self that was "free from bondage to sin"), often preceded by long periods of distress.[29] On the cusp of young womanhood, and in the throes of adversity, they found God's "salvation" through auditory and visionary spiritual experience.

Minty probably felt as these other girls her age did. The religious state that she achieved through solitude, visions, and prayer following her head injury conformed to a similar pattern. What she experienced as a skintight intimacy with God took shape alongside memorable dreams and dramatic visions. The psychological and emotional development of her religious sensibility coincided with the physiological impact of her altered brain to create a powerful sense of amplified, second—or future—sight. Minty was beset by dreams, sometimes terrifying in their vividness, and she likely did not differentiate between the neurological effects of her epileptic seizures and the mysterious gifts of the spirit. She may have felt, when she emerged like a butterfly from its chrysalis that winter, that she was newly debilitated by piercing headaches and unpredictable sleep rhythms but also richly resourced by an internal source of energy. A reduction of her physical ability to remain alert arose alongside an extension of her mental ability to interpret the present and predict the future. Experientially, Minty must have felt a confluence of God's closeness and her mind's expansiveness. Her injury was particular to her circumstances, her visions specific to her psyche, but her choice to accept this altered state of consciousness as religious experience connected her to other spiritually oriented Black girls and young women. With access to a different source of knowledge about the world, and in possession of what she would come to know as a new source of power, she was now distinctly equipped to tackle the questions that haunted her: Why did slavery exist? And (how) would her people be saved?

3

THE WILDERNESS

Let us meet the face of God, seeing that we aren't standing in the traumatic memories of the past alone, but with the breaker of chains and maker of water in the wilderness.

—COLE ARTHUR RILEY, *BLACK LITURGIES*,
@BLACKLITURGIES, INSTAGRAM

If you want to meet Jesus, go in the wilderness, Go in the wilderness, go in the wilderness . . . [Af]flicted sister, go in the wilderness, Go in the wilderness, go in the wilderness.

—TRADITIONAL SPIRITUAL

Entering the wilderness, not for conquest but to seek liberation, requires that we also prepare ourselves to encounter the landscape anew.

—IMANI PERRY, *VEXY THING:
ON GENDER AND LIBERATION*, 2018

S lavery and injury, unease and illness, cast Minty Ross into the wilderness. A place of material hardship, of spiritual difficulty and potentiality, the biblically inspired "wilderness" was well known to Black holy women. Moses and the Israelites had first traversed this foreboding place as they wandered the ancient desert that surrounded Egypt. Drawn from these Bible stories and applied to lived life, the metaphorical wilderness Black women believers entered could be a zone of spiritual temptation and visceral trial, as well as a space of growth and revelation. The wilderness was a Bermuda Triangle for the soul where a person could lose herself. The sojourner here faced real risks and stark stakes. As the divinity scholar Barbara Brown Taylor commented in a conversation with National Public Radio's *On Being* host

Greenbriar Swamp, a space of trial and revelation for Rit Green and her son, is placed here to represent a spiritual wilderness. Blackwater National Wildlife Refuge.

Photo by Perri Meldon, 2023.

Krista Tippett: "Wilderness stories are only good if you make it out alive." There was no guarantee of escape.

Minty barely made it out. The wilderness that she entered at the time of adolescence threatened and simultaneously transformed her life. It was a place of confounding double meanings: negative and positive, dreadful and revelatory, metaphorical and physical. And beyond this, the concept of a "wilderness experience" has two connotations in traditional Black culture that have changed over time, the theologian Delores Williams has explained. Starting around the turn of the twentieth century, African Americans usually represented the wilderness as a psycho-emotional circumstance of suffering, "a near-destruction situation in which God gives personal direction to the believer and thereby helps her make her way out of what she thought was no way," Williams has written. Prior to 1900 and dating back centuries, though, an older sense of the term took a more hopeful cast, emphasizing the physical wilderness as a special space of religious experience described by enslaved people in songs and stories. This earlier understanding of wilderness experience likely traces back to the need for enslaved people to practice their religion secretly, on the edges and in the woods of plantations, lest they be surveilled and punished. Wilderness for them—dense vegetation and tree cover—was an actual site of spiritual refuge. In these natural places out of view, seekers might expect to have profound religious experiences. The wilderness therefore took on symbolic, layered meanings for Black people as a wild place in the world and a wild process of internal change. Through the late nineteenth century at least, Black Christians still expressed a sense of the wilderness as a place to go in search of Jesus. "The wilderness experience, as religious experience, was transforming," according to Williams. And this experiential process, a cultural ritual, included a set structure: "being physically isolated, entering into relationship with God, being healed and changed by Jesus (understood to be the Christ, or Savior), and being motivated to return to the community."[1] The wilderness was many things to the enslaved Black population of Minty's time: a natural area set apart from slaveholders' oversight, a physical place of isolation, an emotional space of vulnerability, and a psychic sphere of suffering, healing, and transformation.

Minty might have died from that blow in the village store. But she didn't. Luck, or fate, or as Tubman would later say, her never-combed head of natural hair, stiff "like a bushel basket," had saved her life.[2] After she was felled like a tree by an overseer's iron weight, Minty entered a period of chronic illness and increased threat of sale. These troubles marked her initiation into her wilderness phase of life. And she could not have known at the time whether she would survive it.

The stars flickered on and off along the Maryland coastline where meteors had made their marks across millennia. The seasons turned. Araminta Ross grew, spending her next five summers tromping damp grasses in her long skirts, observing shorebirds shimmy off water droplets, sneaking time with her mother, and working lands wrested from the

Choptank and Nanticoke peoples who had resided in the area long before it became Dorchester County. After she had rebounded from a life-threatening injury and illness while experiencing the world through an altered mind, she found herself hired out by her owner, Edward Brodess, to "a man for the heaviest kind of out-of-door labor." Araminta's task list went beyond the grueling yet customary field work that Black women were often assigned. She was placed in the hands of a lessee, John Stewart, who first put her to work in his house and later saddled her with outdoor duties customary for grown men. Araminta, a teenaged girl, "drove oxen, carted, ploughed, cut wood and hauled logs, performing Herculean tasks," Emma Telford recorded. "The labor of the horse and the ox, the lifting of barrels and flour and other heavy weights were given to her," Sarah Bradford concurred.[3] Araminta carried out this masculinized type of work in 1830s Maryland, a state of diverse constituencies and labor routines that were multiplying as she matured into young womanhood. Maryland's population included large numbers of Black people with a wide range of skills, especially in the magnetic hub of Baltimore, which, as the historian Seth Rockman has put it, "was perched as the southernmost city in the North and the northernmost city in the South." In Baltimore, approximately eighty miles northwest of Dorchester County, across the Chesapeake Bay, most of the Black population was free, while a significant minority was enslaved. Competition among Black and white, captive and free workers led to tense situations and complex negotiations over terms and wages there. Regular movement of enslaved people escaping from the country to the city and of free Blacks seeking employment in rural as well as urban spaces guaranteed a dynamic labor environment and an active communication network.[4]

Araminta toiled on Stewart's lands for five years, becoming physically stronger, more skilled, and more aware of opportunities that existed within a complicated labor and finance market that extended to Baltimore. Even as she bore the physical weight of wooden barrels and oxen yokes, she also carried the silent burden of her disability. She continued to suffer from pounding headaches. And she would lose consciousness during conversations or in the middle of physical tasks, which meant she was always at serious risk of injuring herself, other people, or the animals she worked with. Sometimes her bouts of semiconsciousness could be as close as fifteen or thirty minutes apart, which would have prolonged her exhausting workdays as she put in more time to complete her jobs. These years of hard physical exertion performed through the fog of chronic pain might have been especially demoralizing for Araminta. She remained ever watchful and afraid of what might happen next. "I was not happy or contented," she later told a reporter in Canada. "[E]very time I saw a white man I was afraid of being carried away. I had two sisters carried away in a chain-gang,—one of them left two children. We were always uneasy."[5]

It was during her middle teenage years that Araminta, anxious and frustrated, recognized an opportunity, then seized upon it. She requested permission to organize her own time and earnings by hiring herself out. In this arrangement, she would schedule her jobs, collect her pay, give most of the money to her owner, and keep a small portion for herself. She would benefit from greater autonomy and the chance to earn cash, while her owner would benefit by ridding himself of the hassle of managing her leases. Her owner would have to agree to this new arrangement, however. He did so only after another white man in the area, to whom Araminta turned for help, guaranteed the agreement by ensuring she would pay.[6] The successful design of this deal tells us much about the teenaged Araminta. It says she was observant, smart, and kept an eye out for opportunity. It says she maintained relationships with people—even white people of the slaveholding classes—who were willing to vouch for her and her family. It says she was an able worker. It says she was trustworthy. And it suggests she had a long-term plan. Now she completed onerous outdoor labor on terms that she herself had negotiated with Stewart, who ran a diversified operation founded by his father, including two-hundred-plus acres of plantation land and hundreds of forested land, as well as mercantile, lumber, and shipbuilding businesses.[7] Araminta may have worked in any or all of these locations, gaining experience and expanded knowledge of various industries as she listened in on exchanges among Stewart, his employees, his customers, and those he enslaved, learning about the politics and economics of her region and broadening her mental map of her surroundings.

Through the pain in her head and the haze of lost time that she could not account for, even to herself, Araminta watched, worked, and waited. Many of her tasks took her to the wooded areas of Stewart's acreage where workers, paid and unpaid, had been assigned to dig a canal for the transport of logs and other valuable materials. Wielding heavy tools, Araminta cut wood and hauled logs.[8] She must have become familiar with tree species and growth cycles, including the sweet gum from which her first cradle had been made. The work was physically demanding but also exhilarating. Araminta had always detested domestic chores in white people's homes—weaving, sweeping, dusting, serving, and rocking babies. She had felt smothered, hampered, and patronized within those walls and, most of all, deeply shamed by the sense of being meanly judged for her appearance and mannerisms. Out in the woods, she could feel more free, widening that notch of autonomy that she had realized she needed and fought for even as a young enslaved child. "She loved the beauty; she loved the quiet," Karen Hill, the current director of the Harriet Tubman Home in upstate New York, has said of Tubman's years in Maryland.[9] At the same time, Araminta would have realized that the natural world she loved was also the scene of her exploitation. She was forced to labor for others here because the land, also a victim, could produce profit for her enslavers. Knowing this, she abided with nature like other enslaved African Americans did—in dual modes of grim recognition and abundant joy.

Araminta's relationship with the land was pragmatically luminous.[10] Despite the toil she did there, she felt an emotional affinity with natural things and may have experienced outdoor time as a balm with healing qualities. The work in nature may have eased the toll of Araminta's disability, too. She was a sensitive person, attuned to her surroundings and appreciative of nature's flourishes. The greenish-brown tint to the waterlogged land may have calmed her; the rustling sounds of the living forest may have soothed her; the pinesap-sharp scent in the air may have energized her; the fastidious habits of busy birds may have charmed her. Ednah Dow Cheney, who knew Tubman later in life, wrote about this outdoor activity: "The blow produced a disease of the brain which was severe for a long time, and still makes her very lethargic. She cannot remain quiet fifteen minutes without appearing to fall asleep. It is not refreshing slumber; but a heavy, weary condition which exhausts her. She therefore loves great physical activity, and direct heat of the sun, which keeps her blood actively circulating."[11] Tubman surely used different words to convey this sensation when she told Cheney about her disability and her enjoyment of the outdoors, but her preference for being outside, even in the context of enslavement, had been established when she was a young child. During this period of her teenage years when she worked for John Stewart, Araminta "learned to love the land, where flora and wildlife reflected seasonal change," one of her contemporary biographers, the historian Catherine Clinton, has written.[12] This love of the land would expand and take on new dimensions as outdoor work led Araminta into reunion with her beloved father.

Ben Ross had spent his childhood, young adulthood, and middle-age years employed for no pay by his owner, the well-to-do landowner Anthony Thompson. Ben lived on Thompson's land in Peter's Neck, an area along the Blackwater River, approximately ten miles from his wife and children, who were based at Edward Brodess's farm. The close-knit Green-Ross family saw each other when they could but for the most part resided in different households.

Over the years, and perhaps owing to innate traits that Araminta might inherit, Ben became especially skilled and experienced at forest work as he serviced Thompson's timber business through lumberjacking. Ben knew how to identify flora, topple trees, transport logs, and carve wood. He was a timberman, logger, and perhaps even a forester who understood the trees' cycles and tried to further their healthy growth. Ben's knack for working in woodlands and with lumber coincided with an economic shift on the Eastern Shore of the Chesapeake Bay. Monied men in this rural part of Maryland were looking for financial opportunities beyond the planting and harvesting of crops on increasingly depleted soils. They invested funds and labor in a surging timber industry and transportation infrastructure of roads and canals.[13]

Ben Ross, who had a skill set suited for this industry, gained his freedom through a provision of Thompson's will. Ben also received a ten-acre parcel of land and a modest home near the Blackwater River upon Thompson's death, pointing, perhaps, to an unusual tie between Ross and his deceased "master."[14] Ben's shift from enslaved man to free man by 1840 situated him among a growing number of free Blacks in rural areas around the commercially salient coastal waterways and in the city of Baltimore. Ben worked as a foreman, was hired by white men with means, and oversaw logging crew employees. Meanwhile, his daughter followed in his footsteps, excelling in woodwork and regularly hiring out her own time.

With his newfound freedom, Ben Ross achieved a long-sought but fragile stability. Now in control of his own time, he took a job with John Stewart, Araminta's employer, even as he likely continued to work for the Thompson family. Ben had a cabin to call his own in Peter's Neck by the early 1840s. His wife, Rit, and a few of their children may have joined him there for a period, as he may have managed to hire out Rit's time from Edward Brodess. Ben also welcomed in his beloved daughter, the ambitious and "uneasy" Araminta. The Tubman biographer and historian Kate Larson calls Ben Ross's cozy home, with its ceramic dishware and brick chimney, the "place where [Harriet] came of age."[15]

Araminta began to work in the woods as a member of her father's crew, the only woman—let alone teenaged girl—among the men. Sarah Bradford wrote of this period: "Frequently she worked with her father, who was a timber inspector, and superintended the cutting and hauling of great quantities of timber for the Baltimore shipyards . . . While engaged with her father, she would cut wood, haul logs, etc." The work was taxing for Araminta, who usually cut "half a cord of wood in a day."[16] Her aching head and blackouts would have been constant reminders of her physical limits. And she was still not free. But Araminta must have delighted in being with her father in the forested marsh and sunny fields as they dragged the logs to transport zones. She may have felt moments of sheer joy working beside Ben Ross and learning from his expertise in the schoolhouse of the woods. As she worked, Araminta absorbed new information about trees, plants, weather, and animal behavior while honing her skills in reading both landscapes and people. She saw her father lead small groups through thick mud beneath dense tree canopy, managing them in the pursuit of a common purpose. "Her father also taught her how to move silently through the forest, imitate bird calls, and use bird sounds to communicate with others. He also taught her how to feel the barks of trees for moss— the moss grew more heavily on the north side of the trees," observed the environmental studies scholar Dorceta Taylor. "The landscape became her classroom," Larson has said. "She learned how to survive in those woods. She learned how to read the night sky."[17] Ben Ross, a woodsman, a Christian, and a foreman, tutored his daughter, who would combine and magnify all three callings. She must have had other teachers, too, as she learned the methods of outdoor survival. The question of who taught Harriet Tubman is an open avenue of inquiry for Larson and a collaborative group of Maryland state and national park researchers tracing her Maryland upbringing. Although their names are not yet known, the certain existence of these additional teachers indicates, once more, that rather than being a lone actor, Tubman was ensconced in community.

When she had reached her late teens or early twenties and had put enough money aside, Araminta did the first of two remarkable things. She purchased a pair of oxen, "worth forty dollars," directing toward her own ends the muscle power of the husbandry animals she had come to know well. And later, in 1848, after she had married, she hired an attorney to research her family history, demonstrating what the historian Dylan Penningroth has called "the legal lives of slaves."[18] We can only wonder how Araminta interacted with the oxen she bought, whether she whispered to them or stroked their broad flanks before or after a stint of work, whether she regretted using the animals to further her own ends, whether she thought back to her days in residence with the corralled sow and piglets, whether she made comparisons to the virtual yoke on her own neck. We do know that with her livestock team in place, Araminta was able to take on more tree work during extra hours that she somehow squeezed into her days. She earned additional income for herself, which she would put to surreptitious use in an investigation of legal records regarding her mother's enslaved status.

Araminta had become a woodswoman with entrepreneurial and legal savvy. She used nature and her knowledge of it to further her goals. In retrospect, she would see this critical bridge time between adolescence and young womanhood spent mainly in the woods as preparatory and even providential. "I was getting fitted for the work the Lord was getting ready for me," she proclaimed.[19]

Existing interviews and dictated biographical sketches do not reveal how Araminta felt about the bodily pain and physical limitations that may have worsened over time, as epileptic seizures tend to increase in frequency and intensity after initial onset.[20] The imperfect reportage of observers indicates that she seemed frustrated and embarrassed by the seizures that left her temporarily unconscious or semiconscious. This may have been the case. But even so, the other Black women of faith we have been following alongside Araminta all experienced some form of illness, pain, and disability as adolescents and young women that they interpreted through spiritual lenses. In other words, in these comparative examples, the women saw illness and disability as milestones along a faith journey. These setbacks allowed God's invisible presence to break through into awareness and sometimes occasioned God's arrival and intervention. Elizabeth, for example, fell into a state of depression after she was beaten and overworked. Her loss of appetite and expectation of death led her to wonder if she was "prepared to

meet [her] maker" and to "desire that the Lord would par-
don [her]." It was only after this phase of psychological and
physical suffering that she had a vision culminating with
God's call to preach. Zilpha Elaw had already converted,
married, begun praying publicly at God's urging after she
heard "God rustling in the tops of the mulberry-trees," when
she experienced her first major illness around the age of
twenty-six. She had a "severe fall" in 1816 leading to internal
injuries that a doctor said she could not survive. But, she
wrote, "God ordered it otherwise than expected." Zilpha
recovered to "resume the work of [her] heavenly Master,
going forth in his great name from day to day, and holding
sweet converse with [her] God, as a man converses with his
friend."[21]

Julia Foote was fifteen years old and newly converted as
of six months when she met with terrible misfortune. A child
in the household "accidentally hit [her] in the eye, causing
the most intense suffering." She lost sight in that eye and
believed that Satan used her disability to taunt her with the
suggestion that her conversion had been counterfeit. Although she prayed, Julia was riddled by doubts, "struggling
and fighting with this inbeing monster." After a year of feeling "every moment of [her] life" was "wretched," she found a
"secret place of prayer" behind the chimney in the garret

and was soon visited by a mysterious woman who prayed with her. The next day, as Julia later wrote, "The glory of God seemed almost to prostrate me to the floor. There was, indeed, a weight of glory resting upon me. I sang with all my heart." She felt that "perfect love took possession" and she "lost all fear." She proclaimed herself "sanctified," by which she meant that she now had the power of the holy spirit within her.[22]

Jarena Lee struggled with years of psychological distress punctuated by suicidal thoughts and leading to a vague physical illness that lasted for three months. She attributed her tribulations to Satan, whom she once saw in her room in the form of a large black dog. During another stretch of physical illness that she describes as stemming from her mental distress, Jarena prayed, "received forgiveness," and learned the meaning of "the entire sanctification of the soul to God." This moment prepared her for hearing God's call to preach around five years later, when she was in her twenties. But her response to that call would be delayed largely due to her sex. Marriage to a pastor and moving with him to a place where she did not have spiritual companionship led to more discontent. God spoke to Jarena in a series of dreams that coincided with her changing health. After one dream, she "fell into a state of general debility, and in an ill state of health" such that she "could not sit up." She prayed on her sickbed and had a dream in which God gave her a "token," the promise of restored health. She prayed, heard God speak in her heart, recovered, and within six years had suffered the loss of five family members, including her husband. The untimely death of Jarena's husband "by his [God's] hand" left her alone to mother a two-year-old and a six-month-old, but it also brought her closer to "the widow's God," she wrote, quoting the Bible. In just over a year, she attained permission from the African Methodist Episcopal Church leader, Richard Allen, to lead prayer meetings and "exhortations." Her response to God's call had begun.[23]

These young women suffered long-term physical or mental illness, or long-term physical disability, that they integrated into their personal narratives of religious growth. Illness and accident appear in their life stories as spiritual warfare—states proactively caused by Satan or retroactively used by Satan to separate them from God. And they viewed their recovery from illness, which varied from temporary reprieve to long-term healing to learning to live with "debility," as Jarena Lee put it, as part of their developing relationship with the god of their belief and the maturation of their faith. Struggling with illness, pain, limited mobility, and pending death were spiritual trials for these women, who drew closer to God and, they report, the Holy Spirit, as a result. Illness was a "wilderness experience" for them, a trial during which they were brought low and found that they needed God's rescue. This sense of a spiritual wilderness, a psychic wild land of wandering, testing, and suffering associated with the Israelites in the Old Testament, surfaces in Julia Foote's memoir, when the unnamed woman who comes to pray with her is described as "an old mother in Israel."[24]

Perhaps Araminta also understood her chronic pain, unpredictable sleep patterns, and recurring periods of debilitation as meaningful features of her spiritual journey. But Araminta did not write a memoir. We are not privy to her direct words. Instead, we read about important moments in her life second- or thirdhand in as-told-to biographical accounts with summarized, paraphrased, and quoted speech rendered in dialect so stylized that we must take seriously the likelihood that her words were only loosely captured. The caverns of Araminta's mind were kept secret over time or omitted by biographers like Sarah Bradford, who admitted to having "rejected," or edited out, "many incidents quite as wonderful as those related in this story."[25] It stands to reason that once Araminta was older, going by a different name, and well known in abolitionist circles, she as well as her biographers left things out, aware that revealing more might expose her most private feelings or test the credulity of readers. Jarena Lee, who did tell her own story, allowing us special, though not total, access to her thoughts, was hyperconscious of how her experiences might come across to the public. She winds down her memoir with the statement: "As to the nature of uncommon impressions, which the reader cannot but have noticed, and possibly sneered at in the course of these pages, they may be accounted for in this way: it is known that the blind have the sense of hearing in a manner much more acute than those who can see: also their sense of feeling is exceedingly fine, and is found to detect any roughness on the smoothest surface, where those who can see can find none. So it may be with such as [I] am."[26] Even though she is unschooled, Lee says (and despite or because of her "debility," we might add), she developed what she interpreted as extraordinary spiritual acuity akin to increased sensory awareness. Did Araminta feel, too, that diminished physical capacity coincided with "exceedingly fine" spiritual antennae, heightening her ability to see, interpret, and project into the future?

Whether or not she sensed that she was now endowed with "uncommon impressions," she was not out of the woods of her wilderness yet.

4

THE DREAMS

We must tap the well of our own collective imaginations,
that we do what earlier generations have done: dream.

—ROBIN D. G. KELLEY, "PREFACE," *FREEDOM DREAMS:
THE BLACK RADICAL IMAGINATION*, 2022

Green trees are bending,
Poor sinners stand a trembling;
The trumpet sounds within my soul;
I ain't got long to stay here.

—"STEAL AWAY TO JESUS," TRADITIONAL SPIRITUAL

When the blackness come/I go where God want.

—QURAYSH ALI LANSANA, "TRUTH," *THEY SHALL RUN:
HARRIET TUBMAN POEMS*, 2004

At twenty years old, Araminta Ross lived as both an ordinary and extraordinary enslaved woman. She had experienced forced separation from parents and siblings, withstood physical assault at the hands of an overseer, suffered serial illnesses stemming from the impositions of her captivity, and learned to labor indoors and out. She had also taken partial control of her own time and emerged alive from a physical and psychological wilderness. And she was beginning to consider what it would mean to live out a life in this place of bondage, forming a family in a context of suffering as her parents had. In what may have been a period of emotional searching, she found a mate. Around the year 1844 when she was approximately twenty-two, Araminta wed John Tubman, a free Black man in the area who was approximately ten years her senior and probably a farm laborer.[1] Little else is known about John, and perhaps that is how his wife later wanted it. Biographers and historians have strained to make sense of this first marriage and to represent the feelings the couple had for each other, at times suggesting that John Tubman must have been in love to marry a woman who would give birth to enslaved children.[2] The historical record is silent, though, on John Tubman's feelings and only whispers of Araminta's. The women writers to whom an older Harriet Tubman would later tell her story had mere scraps to offer about Tubman's young conjugal life. Ednah Dow Cheney wrote of the union: "She was married about 1844 to a free colored man named John Tubman, but never had any children."[3] Emma Telford related: "About this time she married a free colored man named John Tubman but she had no children."[4] Araminta, for her part, seems to have been attached to her new husband. She may have felt that her marriage was a rite of passage into adulthood, for it was in this period that she changed her name. No longer did she wish to be called Araminta or Minty, or to be known by her father's surname, Ross. She replaced these names, taking her husband's last name, Tubman, and her mother's first name, Harriet.

Names were important to enslaved people, who often had to bear appellations imposed by enslavers and were typically denied the use of surnames that would identify them as members of families. In her twenties, Harriet Tubman had entered a new season of life punctuated by her decision to rename herself. In doing so, she took an action more typical of formerly enslaved people *after* they had escaped the South. Perhaps this action casts a glow of foreshadowing over her story. Whether or not Araminta already sensed she would someday run, with this move she shed the name she had carried over decades spent in bondage and claimed a new identity. By adopting "Harriet," she likely expressed affection for the mother who had repeatedly brought her back from the brink of serious illness and injury. By taking "Tubman," she claimed her role as a spouse in a place and culture in which a Black enslaved woman had to receive permission from an owner to wed. Furthermore, even if that allowance to marry was granted, the enslaved woman entered a conjugal union viewed as a person who would remain violable by men not her husband. Harriet's new name signaled an enduring connection to her natal family and also announced her intention to be respected as a wife—a constituent part of a new family formed with her spouse. Through her act of self-naming, Harriet Tubman expressed an individual selfhood that was at the same time enwrapped in the ribbons of kinship. Her chosen name, bold to the ear due to its robust consonants, revealed again twin aspects of her character that had been evident since childhood: personal dignity and familial devotion.

———

When Harriet and John Tubman were newlyweds, the young couple likely lived apart much of the time. Still, they tried to build a life in the shadow of slavery, with the next long day of hard work always on the horizon and fear of the chain gang ever clouding Harriet's mind. She continued to toil in the woods, plagued by headaches and blackouts and disturbed by visions and dreams. Whenever she closed her eyes, Harriet saw white men on horseback hunting her people, hunting her. These horror shows in Harriet's mind caused her to "start up at night with the cry 'Oh, they're coming, they're coming, I must go,'" Sarah Bradford wrote, quoting her. Harriet's dreams recurred and expanded in this period of her life, blurring into additional scenes that combined fear, anxiety, and wishes deferred. "'And all that time, in my dreams and visions,'" she would later tell Bradford, "'I seemed to see a line, and on the other side of that line were green fields, and lovely flowers, and beautiful white ladies, who stretched out their arms to me over the line, but I couldn't reach them . . . I always fell before I got to the line."[5]

In Harriet's recurring dreams, which she linked to her visions, suggesting that she experienced both as similar departures from the clearly conscious waking world, she ran for her life under chase by the demon Slavery's human agents. Her dream imagery of green fields and white ladies standing on the other side of a border were psychological projections about her state of captivity, her notions of freedom, and her fear that she would never cross over, likely spurred or intensified by her temporal lobe epilepsy. These daymares and night dreams were also laced with latent religious symbolism. The four horsemen of the apocalypse thundered through her waking visions. And her overnight dreams of white figures beckoning from across a boundary share visual symbols in common with the conversion vision of the preacher "Old" Elizabeth. Elizabeth had been twelve and enslaved when she watched a spirit guide dressed in white lead her to the edge of an "awful pit" and then to the threshold of "heaven's door," where "millions of glorified spirits in white robes" appeared on the other side.[6] For Elizabeth and perhaps for Harriet, too, dreams of hell and heaven were simultaneously dreams of slavery and freedom with pointed geographical features: borders, edges, and sinkholes.

To Harriet Tubman, these hellish dreams felt real and even cautionary, but to John Tubman, they may have seemed overwrought. Spending time with Harriet, who may have appeared like a person obsessed, could have been worrying and frustrating for him. According to Bradford, "her husband called her a fool" and downplayed Harriet's trepidations.[7] It is possible that Bradford's choice of language here would not have been the same as Harriet's if we could hear her tell it, but it is nevertheless likely that this statement reflected disagreement between Harriet and her spouse about how to make sense of frightening mental images. The record does not indicate whether John Tubman was a religious man. It is possible that he held views distinct from Harriet's and did not think, as she did, that God could speak to a person through spiritual means. If John did downplay or even ridicule Harriet's beliefs, he would not have been the only spouse of a devout Black woman to do so. Julia Foote, who had married and moved to Boston following her conversion at age fifteen, expressed that after she became "sanctified" and was nearly knocked down by the "glory of God," her husband said she was "getting more crazy every day." Zilpha Elaw warned women readers of her memoir not to become "unequally yoked with unbelievers" and confided that her husband "resolved to use every means to induce me to renounce my religion."[8]

Harriet Tubman's active mind kept producing alarming scenes that may have created tensions with her husband and increased her own anxiety, pushing her to feel that she must respond to these dreams—and soon. Among her dreams in these years was a variation of the white-ladies-over-the-borderline vignette with a striking new element. Sarah Bradford writes about this period in Tubman's life: "She declares that before her escape from slavery, she used to dream of flying over fields and towns, and rivers and mountains, looking down upon them 'like a bird,' and reaching at last a great fence, or sometimes a river, over which she would try to fly." At this point in the biography, Bradford quotes Tubman: "'But I appeared like I wouldn't have the strength, and just as I was sinking down, there would be ladies all dressed in white over there, and they would put out their arms and pull me across.'"[9]

The naturalistic setting for this dream predominates. The landscape is both background and dramatic element as Tubman surveys an array of ecological zones true to Maryland, a state of varied topography from the large coastal plain (where Harriet had been born in the southern region), to the rocky piedmont zone, to the rising swells of the Appalachians. It is doubtful, though, that Harriet had ever seen the high hills and cavernous streams to the northeast, let alone Sugarloaf Mountain closer to the fall line where waterfalls marked a change in the land leading to the Blue Ridge peaks to the northwest.[10] Harriet was familiar with waterfowl, blue crabs, and eastern oysters, not grassland birds, cold-water fish, and bats. But she had probably heard about these other regions, microclimates, and animal in-habitants of the state from the talk of free Black sailors or on-foot laborers traveling to and from Baltimore or free Black workers at Stewart's timber operation. The far-reaching topographical range of her dream landscape, from agricul-tural fields to rugged mountains, suggests this scene unfolded on an imagination-enhanced map rather than a strictly ac-curate map of Tubman's own local environs. In this version of the borderline dream, Tubman again encounters a geo-graphical barrier, here materialized as a fence or river that stands between a state of freedom and a state of slavery. The "white ladies" on the free side seem to be human, and Brad-ford reads them as such, but they are also akin to the angels and spirit guides represented in other Black holy women's dreams. The feeling of "sinking down" in the dream is the descent again into bondage, or the inferno. Harriet Tubman would make this analogy directly in the mid-1850s when she was a veteran escapee and safely away in Canada. "I think slavery is the next thing to hell," she said.[11]

But there is a difference in the details of this later ver-sion in the borderline dream series as reported by Bradford. Significantly, as Harriet navigates this dream soon before her escape, she does so "like a bird," language that is attrib-uted to her as a quote in Bradford's biography. Perhaps even more important than her change of names in this phase of

This contemporary embroidery by the historian and needle artist Harriet Hyman Alonso portrays Harriet Tubman growing from an enslaved girl to a free woman, leading others to liberation. Tubman's famous quotation mirrors the depicted transformation. Alonso writes about this work in 2023: "The piece can be looked at as an example of American folk art using 18th and 19th century embroidered samplers as inspiration."

Image reproduced with permission from Harriet Hyman Alonso.

life, Harriet has shifted shape in this symbolic imaginary. She is not the same human woman with feet tethered to the ground being chased by human men on horseback. She is instead an air being with a bird's high vantage point even as she carries the weight of her own personal and communal human history. As a dream bird, Harriet can rise above her surroundings and see farther than a person on foot (or a person awake) could manage. She gains a panoramic perspective and the mental ability to penetrate dimensions. She can see the changing forms of the land, the good intentions of the ladies, and the physical obstacles arrayed below. Even as her heart races with foreknowledge of the thundering horsemen always chasing her in a frightening loop, she can feel the wind beneath her fledgling wings.

Harriet probably interpreted these dreams as divinely inspired, seeing them through her ever-present spiritual lens. The bird imagery loosely ties her dreams, and perhaps her sense of self in this period, to the words of other Black women believers who drew on the Bible to describe their experiences of marginalization. Elizabeth, who began to lead informal prayer assemblies at age forty-two after she was freed, faced criticism from church elders for teaching the gospel as a woman. Drawing on a verse in the book of Jeremiah, "Mine heritage is unto me as a speckled bird, the birds round about are against her," Elizabeth compared herself to a bird when reflecting on this trying period: "I felt that I was despised on account of this gracious calling, and was looked upon as a speckled bird by the ministers to whom I looked for instruction." Zilpha Elaw wrote similarly of her feeling of isolation among the family she served: "Amongst them I dwelt as a speckled bird."[12] Harriet Tubman, also physically marked for ill treatment due to her race, caste, and gender, likewise associated herself with a bird as she dreamt of escape from her predicament. Elizabeth's and Zilpha's bird was "speckled," or darkened by spots to signify their blackness, femaleness, and oddness by societal standards. Harriet's dream bird, in contrast, was probably snow-white in color, a detail grounded in her experience of outdoor work in marshy pine forests.

While growing up on the Eastern Shore of the Chesapeake Bay and working the waterlogged fields and woodlands there, Harriet would have seen and heard all manner of birds nesting, soaring, and calling: majestic, gold-beaked eagles, flocks of Canada and snow geese, elegant tundra swans, and ducks with black, blue, teal, or white wings.[13] Among these myriad avian types, the egret is most likely to have inspired Harriet's dream bird, as a species she might have called up from the subconscious depths of her memory.[14] Egrets were common on the porous terrain of Maryland wetlands but visually striking with their snowdrop tufts and thin gray or black legs. Their graceful movement overhead or on the ground, where they stepped and pecked lightly enough that they barely left physical traces, surely caught Harriet's eye and held her imagination. *If only I could be one of these creatures and fly far away from here*, she may

A great egret stands and casts a wary eye. Unidentified artist (French, active ca. 1520–70), *Great Egret (Ardea alba)*, ca. 1554–64; watercolor, black ink, and white lead pigment over black chalk on ivory paper; 15 3/8 x 10 3/4 inches.

Gift of Nathaniel H. Bishop, 1889.10.1.12, New-York Historical Society.

have thought while staring out over the swamps. Commonly in Harriet's dream, her flight nearly fails, turning into a nightmare.

But this time, in a different version of the recurring dream, Harriet has supernatural help, the outstretched arms of the ladies. Notice that the simple "white ladies" in a previous account of the dream series become the embellished "ladies in white dresses" in this rendition. The ladies are garbed in spiritual attire, becoming spirit figures rather than flesh-and-blood women. And Harriet in her pure white wings is a spirit figure too, a once flesh-and-blood Black woman now robed in divine light. The clear air through which she soars can be read as a spiritual plane existing beyond geographical reality. The bird she becomes in her dreams is not therefore bound by societal rules; it is instead empowered to break free of them. The analysis of the religious historian Alexis Wells-Oghoghomeh adds yet another intriguing dimension to this suggestion that the ladies and the bird are spirit beings—or spiritual versions of those who would be key actors in any actual border crossing attempt: Harriet and her female helpers. In her study of West and Central African influences on enslaved women's spiritual beliefs in Georgia, Wells-Oghoghomeh found that animals, and especially birds, figured prominently. The jaybird was singled out for playing a role in the creation and destruction of the earth, while birds as a type occupied a revered status because of their flying capabilities. Enslaved people associated birds with omens and messages. And birds signified a particularly feminine spiritual connection through associations with a sacred female society and with motherhood and fertility.[15] When Harriet dreamed of herself as a bird, she may have been subconsciously drawing on multiple and culturally diverse associations: the egrets of her homeland; the tie between the color white and the spiritual realm in her Christian faith culture; and the links among birds, messages, and women that may have existed in her community's African-descended folk culture and cosmology.

If Harriet's physical preparation for future feats of escape took shape through woodwork, as she would later indicate, her mental preparation may have been forged through dreamwork in this same period. But her husband would not journey with her through this demanding psychological terrain. Whether or not John Tubman was as skeptical of Harriet's views about the meanings of her dream and what lay ahead as Bradford related, he could not have fully understood his wife's position. He was free; she was bound. He was male; she was female. Only she was owned by another, and only she could give birth to property. The moral question of how a system as vile as slavery could exist had plagued her since childhood. Her dreams, her circumstance, and her overwhelmingly fraught thoughts would not give her license to accept the vicissitudes of daily life. Instead, she looked forward, across the landscape of her future, fixated on what might lie ahead. Harriet seemed to dwell on two planes at once: her present reality and a future possibility where she or another loved one could plummet to greater depths in the pit of human bondage. She knew the brand of slavery she experienced was nearly unbearable, but also that things could be far worse. Her sisters had been exiled into a harsher Deep South slavery, leaving behind lost children and grieving family members. Harriet mourned these sisters, feared their fate would also be hers, and lamented the forlorn state of their babies. The repetition and intensity of Harriet's dreams in the 1840s may have told her a crisis was coming.

In the winter of 1848–49, Harriet's mental distress was compounded by a vague physical sickness. Perhaps her susceptibility to falling ill had been increased by her mounting worry. She was around twenty-six years old, still married to John, and working then on the Caroline County plantation of Dr. Anthony Thompson, a son of her father's former owner. While hiring out her own time, she was earning approximately fifty to sixty dollars per year (around $1,736 at the floor of that range in today's dollars) for her legal owner, Edward Brodess.[16] Sickness weakened her yet again, leading to the need for a long recovery in what seemed to be a cementing pattern of ill health. It is not clear whether she spent these miserable weeks in a cabin, cellar, or attic on Thompson's grounds, or if her father, Ben, may have facilitated her stay in his own cabin. Brodess, who already felt he made too little from Harriet's labor, began to search for a buyer to take the sickly woman off his balance sheet. From Christmas through March of that year, Harriet suffered physically and psychologically, not knowing if she would rebound and regain her health. Sarah Bradford wrote of this arduous season in Harriet's life: "As she recovered from this long illness, a deeper religious spirit seemed to take possession of her than she had ever experienced before. She literally 'prayed without ceasing.'"[17]

From where she lay on yet another sickbed, Harriet Tubman knew Edward Brodess aimed to sell her and sought God's intervention. "'I didn't do nothing but pray for old master,'" Bradford quotes her as saying, "'Oh Lord convert old master. Change that man's heart and make him a Christian.' Soon I heard as soon as I was able to move I was to be sent with my brothers in the chain-gang to the far south. Then I changed my prayer, and I said, 'Lord, if you ain't never going to change that man's heart kill him Lord and take him out of the way . . .' Next thing I knew I heard he was dead, and he died just as he had lived, a wicked, bad man."[18]

Edward Brodess passed away on March 7 of that spring, at age forty-seven. Harriet had prayed for God to step in, and he had seemed to listen. The very act of praying, and the contents of those prayers, reveal her thought processes. She believed that she and her god shared a moral vision—of right and wrong and of justice. She believed she could speak to God and be heard. And to her mind, her belief was confirmed when God seemed to judge her "wicked" master as deserving of the ultimate punishment. But when Harriet learned of Brodess's death, she sank into self-doubt, feeling guilty about her request and wishing she could "bring back that poor soul." She now faced a moral dilemma that only intensified her religiosity.[19]

Tubman recalled, as quoted by Bradford, that as she gradually resumed activity that spring following her owner's death: "I prayed all the time . . . about my work, everywhere; I was always talking to the Lord. When I went to the horse-trough to wash my face, and took up the water in my hands, I said, 'Oh Lord, wash me, make me clean.' When I took up the towel to wipe my face and my hands, I cried, 'Oh Lord, for Jesus' sake, wipe away all my sins!' When I took up the broom and began to sweep, I groaned, 'Oh, Lord whatsoever sin there be in my heart, sweep it out, Lord, clear and clean; but I can't pray no more for poor old master.'"[20] She had given up praying for her dead owner. She instead prayed for the cleansing of her soul. In this period of fervent prayer, she may have achieved what other devout Black women called "sanctification" or "holiness," a state of "spiritual perfection" combined with "the indwelling of the Holy Spirit."[21] Jarena Lee, for example, had struggled for years with suicidal thoughts and with physical illness, which she attributed to "the work of Satan." Through these trials she prayed until, around the age of twenty-one, she reached what she described as "sanctification," the giving over of her whole soul to God.[22] Like the Black women memoirists in her time who would call themselves sanctified, usually after a prolonged mental or physical illness, Harriet may have emerged convinced she knew God's will for her life and committed to following it.

On the heels of these dramatic happenings—her long illness, her owner's death, her desperate prayers and insistent dreams—Harriet's risk intensified. The death of Brodess did not prevent an impending sale of the young woman but instead sent the Brodess family spinning into financial disarray that endangered the well-being and stability of all the Black people they owned. The chatter slipped from enslavers' tongues to enslaved people's ears across the marshy miles of the Eastern Shore. Edward Brodess's widow, Eliza Brodess, was seeking legal recourse to sell people to cover the debts of the estate. Every young person in Harriet's family was vulnerable. They could be yoked to a chain gang. They could be sold down the river. They could become like those dearly departed sisters, lost souls never seen by their families again. John Tubman, according to Sarah Bradford's reportage, may have at first downplayed the rumors and characterized Harriet's worry as overreaction. If so, he would have been proven wrong. In June of 1849, Eliza Brodess advertised the availability of Harriet Tubman's niece, also called Harriet, to potential buyers in the local newspaper; in September, she posted an ad to sell another of Harriet's nieces, Kessiah. While these transactions did not go through, Eliza Brodess did sell Kessiah's sister Harriet and her baby Mary Jane, in June of 1850.[23] Harriet must have trembled with enraged fear upon hearing this news, convinced, perhaps, that her visions were materializing. The loss of these family members was devastating. And any one of them could be next on the demon Slavery's auction block.

Autumn, the season of turning, was again a time of great change for Harriet. It was fall, in the year 1849, when she decided to flee with her younger brothers: Ben, aged twenty-five, and Henry, aged nineteen.[24] The story of their evening escape has been recounted many times, by Harriet herself before audiences small and large, by her biographers in the nineteenth century, and by scholars, filmmakers, and novelists in our own time. "She held a hurried consultation with her brothers," Sarah Bradford wrote, "in which she so wrought upon their fears, that they expressed themselves as willing to start that very night, for that far North, where, could they reach it in safety, freedom awaited them."[25]

Strict secrecy must be maintained, as speaking aloud of

their plans could result in cruel consequences. The siblings might be whipped, confined in a building on a plantation, locked in the county jail, or immediately sold away. Enslavers and patrollers were always on the alert for unusual behavior. Fellow enslaved people might be induced to give them up. Harriet set out with Ben and Henry, but soon the men balked. Telford recounted, in words less compassionate than Harriet herself was likely to have used in describing the little brothers for whom she had cared when they were young and with whom she had watched the falling stars: "Harriet and her brothers now turned their faces northward; but the Men were faint hearted, fearing to face the unknown terror and soon turned back."[26] Days into the journey, the brothers could not carry on. They knew that people left behind counted on them. They felt the way forward was treacherous. They realized recapture was likely. They suspected suffering lay in wait.

How did they tell their sister that they felt compelled to go back? Surely, they did not want to leave her in the deep woods of uncertain night. Their sister was slight in stature, beset by visions, and prone to dropping suddenly into states of unconsciousness. How many times already had she suffered seizures as the trio met at a rendezvous point, made their way mile after mile, slogged through thick mud and leaves, crept and careened beneath pine boughs? How many times had the younger men been there to catch Harriet as she fell, to hold her head above the mud as she sank? Surely, Ben and Henry begged her or even commanded her to return home with them, to take the path back to known captivity over the road forward to unknown fate.

Which was the right course of action, to continue or turn back? What would God expect of her, Harriet must have wondered. Did she think this temptation in the woods had been manufactured by Satan, like other Black holy women, Jarena Lee and Zilpha Elaw, had believed was the case when they faced adversities too strange, in their minds, to be solely of this world? Or did Harriet believe that her dreams and visions, linked to her inward, spiritual eye, had led her to this spot and this decision? Surely, her mind was wild with competing thoughts and frightening doubts as the spectral sound of horse hooves thundered in her pounding head. In this moment, sharp and stiff, or prolonged and plaintive, Harriet Tubman fully met her wilderness experience. Like the illnesses she had endured since childhood, this period of intense difficulty and confusion would last for years. For her, the greatest test, the harshest trial apart from lifelong enslavement, was separation from those she loved. She was damned no matter what she did. Her entire existence was dilemma. Perhaps, for long seconds in those woods on that September night, she froze on the precipice between past

THREE HUNDRED DOLLARS REWARD.

RANAWAY from the subscriber on Monday the 17th ult., three negroes, named as follows: HARRY, aged about 19 years, has on one side of his neck a wen, just under the ear, he is of a dark chestnut color, about 5 feet 8 or 9 inches hight; BEN, aged aged about 25 years, is very quick to speak when spoken to, he is of a chestnut color, about six feet high; MINTY, aged about 27 years, is of a chestnut color, fine looking, and about 5 feet high. One hundred dollars reward will be given for each of the above named negroes, if taken out of the State, and $50 each if taken in the State. They must be lodged in Baltimore, Easton or Cambridge Jail, in Maryland.

ELIZA ANN BRODESS,
Near Bucktown, Dorchester county, Md.
Oct. 3d, 1849.

☞The Delaware Gazette will please copy the above three weeks, and charge this office.

Runaway advertisement for Minty, Ben, and Harry [Henry]. This notice of reward for the recapture of Harriet Tubman and her brothers was placed by Eliza Ann Brodess in the *Cambridge Democrat*, Cambridge, Maryland, October 3, 1849.

Courtesy of Jay and Susan Meredith, Bucktown Village Foundation.

and future, between community and isolation, wondering, fearing, what lay ahead *and* behind her and her brothers.

The siblings had lasted on the run for nearly two weeks, living off whatever provisions they had managed to bring and the flowing streams and native foods of a woodland preparing for winter's pause. Harriet knew how to identify edible plants in the autumnal forest. She may have spotted narrow-leaved sunflower, wintergreen, or swamp blackberry that Indigenous people of the Chesapeake pine woods had relied on for generations.[27] Nevertheless, the siblings must have been hungry and exhausted, hiking long, dark hours for days. Already, those who owned them and those who stood to earn cash from recapturing them (from bounty hunters to newspaper printers) had begun the chase. "Three Hundred Dollars Reward," the advertisement placed by Eliza Ann Brodess began. "Ran away from the subscriber on Monday the 17th . . . three negroes, named as follows." The ad named Henry (as "Harry") first, then Ben, then "MINTY, aged about 27 years . . . of a chestnut color, fine looking, and about 5 feet high."[28]

Recapture could mean brutal beatings and immediate sale far from home. But perhaps giving themselves up could reduce the intensity of the coming punishments. At some point along the way, Ben and Henry decided to retreat, returning to the known world where they bore responsibilities as husbands, fathers, and sons. Harriet stuck with them, surely terrified of attempting to make such a dangerous journey on her own.

But there would be a next time, and soon. Within days of

being back on the Thompson plantation, Harriet made her second break, dismissing the wishes of her brothers, the expressed view of her husband, and the likely desire of her parents to keep her close. One evening in late September or early October, Harriet threw herself into the arms of the woods.

What were the qualities of these wetland woods into which Harriet Tubman surged? Thick stands of loblolly pines, interspersed with hardwood trees (oak, maple, black gum, and sweet gum), sank their roots into damp soils edging brackish swamp waters.[29] This was the home or stopping place of fox squirrels, bald eagles, and box turtles, of migrating birds seeking to winter, and red foxes aiming to hunt.[30] Eastern Shore forests may have been hosts to "wolf trees," too, aged specimens whose lives had begun long before the woods grew around them, evidenced by a wide girth of open-umbrella branches.[31] The soil in these woods would have been seeping, spongy, and puddled, giving way to sunken streams and turning to clay and silt near the marsh.[32] Harriet would have to step through wet dirt and tree droppings, trying to avoid water snakes and sweet gum pods. This landscape was a soundscape, too, as Harriet would have navigated mostly by ear within the thin light afforded by a crisp fall moon. Her terror must have been paramount. But her god would have been present. The woods, to her, would have been brimming with celestial and terrestrial spirits, stocked with guides and defenders in the forms of stars, plants, and trees. Together with these living things and energetic entities, Harriet Tubman "co-authored" a new landscape and waterscape of emancipation.[33] "Tubman's dreams," as the Black feminist geographer Loren Cahill has put it, "gave birth to freedom maps."[34]

This crossing of the borderline of Harriet's dreams would be the first of many. "When going on these journeys," Ednah Cheney wrote about Tubman decades later, "she often lay alone in the forests all night. Her whole soul was filled with awe of the mysterious Unseen presence, which thrilled her with such depths of emotion, that all other care and fear vanished."[35] If these coastal woods had served as a hideout for Rit and a workplace for Ben, they would become that and much more to their runaway daughter, Harriet—a church, a school, a battlefield, a transitory home, and a sanctuary where mounted hunters had no purchase.

THE MIDNIGHT STARS

Photographs by Amani Willett. Introduction by Tiya Miles.
Captions by Lucy Jackson based on the research of Amani Willett.

═══════

Harriet Tubman lived in dynamic relationship to varied and changing environments. Her landscapes were interior as well as exterior, chosen as well as compulsory. This book attempts to capture those many environments through words. Visuals, though, can convey hidden dimensions of environmental contexts, allowing us to imagine Tubman in her material worlds and enabling us to make connections between her landscapes and our own. Toward this end, we present selected art photographs by the contemporary artist Amani Willett that reflect and enlarge themes of this book while illuminating pivotal moments of Harriet Tubman's grounded life journey.

Amani Willett is a descendant of Quakers. He created his series *The Underground Railroad: Hiding in Place* to explore personal and national history in relation to sites in the North and South. His original series, exhibited in 2015, included nineteen color images and six black-and-white images taken between the years 2010 and 2015. Willett writes that these images "could be considered a family history of sorts. My mother is black and my father white and were both raised as Quakers—a religious organization whose members were deeply invested in the abolitionist movement." Over time, the series became "an investigation of the way history, memory, and mythology have been etched into Underground Railroad sites," he explains, concluding that "the way we, as a society, have chosen to remember or reconstruct our past is just as informative and important as the truth."

We reproduce six evocative images from Amani Willett's *Underground Railroad* series here, inviting you to imagine Tubman's flights across land and water, through spiritual and psychological realms, and across time in our cultural memories—and then to question and stretch those imaginings. The first image presents us with a road flanked by a prominent tree and fertile fields, eliciting, perhaps, Tubman's childhood years on plantations and farms in rural Maryland.

This photo may also bring to mind analogies made in the text between Tubman as a sheltering figure and the tree as a sheltering thing in the human cultural imagination, prompting awareness of the thin boundary between reliance and exploitation. The second picture, a close-up of a wooden church pew, conjures the notion of faith as psychological sanctuary. The red cushion on the pew might signify religious passion, or, alternatively, the violence Tubman observed and endured in a region and time of hyper-expressive Christian identity. The third image, a preserved antique dining area, reminds us of the dangerous yet unpredictable domestic realms that Tubman navigated, of her presence as a captive child within kitchens, parlors, and bedrooms of enslavers, as well as her presence within antislavery haven-households. The pitcher of water on the table poses an implicit question about how we are to read the public embrace of triumphant Underground Railroad stories—as a vessel half empty, or half full? The fourth photograph draws us into a visual tangle of thin trees in an autumn woodland, simulating a feeling of bewilderment for us while evoking Tubman's first trip from forest to freedom. The fifth image, in which trees arch over a churning stream, could represent Tubman's flight through and over waterways. This shot, special in the series for our purposes, corresponds directly with Tubman's personal geography, as it features Maryland's Choptank River. The image also leads us to ask: What truths remain submerged when we see Harriet Tubman as a fantasy hero who walked on water? The sixth and final image, showing a bright white stone partly obscured by wild greenery at the Mason–Dixon line, brings us full circle, representing Tubman's troubling childhood as a "neglected weed" as well as her textured legacy as "our rock."

Amani Willett reminds us that even as we recall the sites of the Underground Railroad, we risk confusing mythology for history. Nevertheless, entertain for a moment a blurring of that categorical border. The number of pictures chosen for this insert—six—corresponds with the Tubman adage that God had delivered her through six troubles and so could be counted on in the seventh. A space is held in reserve here for our own future scene of trouble, in the wish that we, like Tubman, will be guided by the light.

SITE OF THE CHRISTIANA RIOT

The tree enmeshed in vines reaches up to the
sky and down into the ground, anchored to the soil
where residents sheltered freedom seekers with
firearms in 1851. Christiana, Pennsylvania.

WILLETT CHURCH

The secret door behind the pew at Bialystoker Synagogue,
formerly the Willett Street Methodist Episcopal Church,
opens into a passageway leading to an attic, a holy haven
on the trail to freedom. New York, New York.

VICKERS TAVERN

John Vickers was a long-standing Pennsylvania abolitionist, Quaker, and potter. Vickers's farmhouse was known as the Great Central Station of the Underground Railroad in Chester County because freedom seekers hid in the basement (behind the pictured door), which was also used as a pottery shop. Exton, Chester County, Pennsylvania.

OVERNIGHT SHELTER

These tangled woods sheltered freedom seekers
in 1847. Property of the Wayside Inn, owned by the
Alcott family. Concord, Massachusetts.

RED BRIDGES

This stream flows into the Choptank River, along
one of Harriet Tubman's Underground Railroad routes
to Sandtown, Delaware. Greensboro, Maryland.

MASON–DIXON LINE MARKER

Once self-emancipators like Tubman crossed
this geographical line, they considered themselves,
and were considered by many others in the North,
to be free. Maryland/Pennsylvania border.

5

THE FLIGHT

I'll fly away, oh, Glory
I'll fly away.

—"I'LL FLY AWAY," TRADITIONAL SPIRITUAL

I dream in bird clan
A language that ties me
To what is and what was.

—CIRCE STURM, "FREEDOM MOST RANKLES,"
SAY, LISTEN: WRITING AS CARE, 2023

There is nothing like the beautiful free forest.

—EDMONIA LEWIS, AFRO-OJIBWE SCULPTOR,
INTERVIEW, *BROKEN FETTER*, 1865

Harriet Tubman took wing. At the time of her permanent escape in the autumn of 1849, she had lived around twenty-seven years as the claimed property of others. But freeing herself meant losing the people and places she loved, and perhaps left her wondering why her god would exact such a price. According to her as-told-to biographers, Harriet communicated her intentions to family members before she acted. She is described as wearing a sunbonnet, traversing the grounds of Thompson's plantation, and singing these words loud enough to ring across the acreage: "When that old chariot comes, I'm going to leave you; I'm bound for the promised land."

What did Harriet Tubman's soaring voice sound like? This is difficult for us to know. She spoke in a regional Black accent that biographers in her time failed to render respectfully and accurately on the page. Sarah Bradford wrote that Tubman sang an old hymn, which she had used as a message song during an escape, in a "sweet and simple Methodist air." Bradford said, in describing another Tubman song of this type, "the air sung to these words was so wild, so full of plaintive minor strains, and unexpected quavers" that Bradford "would defy any white person to learn it."[1] From these imperfect descriptions, we might glean that Tubman possessed a striking vocal range and an enthralling singing voice that could reproduce traditional Anglo Methodist sounds as well as improvisational tones influenced by her African diasporic roots. What was strange and foreign to Bradford's ear would have been familiar to enslaved Black people across the South in their small churches and forested "shout" circles. Harriet must have had a melodious voice, given her apparent love of song and repeated practice of the form. She must have had a forceful voice that captivated and carried. When she sang the words "I'm sorry I'm going to leave you, Farewell, oh Farewell; But I'll meet you in the morning . . . On the other side of Jordan, Bound for the promised land," as she moved outside the captive spaces of her relatives, she must have pierced their listening hearts.

Harriet's goodbye song about the promised land, like her recurring dream of flying toward the borderline, reflected her persistent awareness of geography. She intended to traverse a boundary, to cross to an "other" side. And this "other" space was both physical and allegorical. She was headed to the American North and to the biblical wilderness of old. Hers was to be a physical and spiritual journey. This new place had been "promised" to her by God just as a land of freedom had been promised to the Israelites by Jehovah. Aspirational and hopeful, this melody was also a dirge full of regret and melancholy. Through the lyrics, Harriet apologized. Family was one of her two core values. The other was following what she perceived as the voice of God. No longer traveling with her brothers, she had to leave all her relatives behind as she embarked on this long walk into mystery. Her husband, John, had been against this course of action. Her mother, Rit, her father, Ben, her siblings, cousins, nieces, nephews, friends who acted like kin, and even her oxen would all remain on this side of the border, a virtual hellscape.

This was the personal and spiritual wilderness Harriet had to navigate even as she maneuvered through the physical woodlands of eastern Maryland. She made this leap with precious little information, "with almost no knowledge (of) the north, having only heard of Pennsylvania And New Jersey," Emma Telford would recount.[2] But although she trudged through the trees in isolation that long first night,

Harriet was not alone in spirit. The remembered voices of her brothers from the last time she trod this trail may have reverberated in the stillness around her. The protection of her personal god must have enveloped her. The shedding pines and oak trees surely stood with her. The wild plants would have nourished her. The North Star, she would later proclaim, ably guided her. And the plans she had laid to get this far on an unpredictable, dangerous quest included human helpers, too, some positively identified and some still unknown because of the clandestine nature of an effective freedom network.

In the late 1990s and early 2000s, 150 years after Tubman's escape, the Underground Railroad—or the secret web of activists pledged to aid freedom seekers—surged in public popularity. Historic homes, churches, and barns across the Northeast and Midwest announced their status as Underground Railroad stops or stations. Books detailing the brave actions and intricate hidden connections of stationmasters and conductors appeared on bookshop and library shelves. Public panels featured descendants of those who had helped and those who had run away. Even the Home and Garden Television channel (HGTV) departed from its typical design-oriented programming to produce a show titled *Homes of the Underground Railroad* during Black History Month in 2002. Partly a result of this surge of interest in an antebellum social movement, and partly responsible for it, was the wide-spread dissemination of the idea, now discredited in academic circles, that enslaved people had designed quilts with coded messages keyed to escape plans. In *Hidden in Plain View: A Secret Story of Quilts and the Underground Railroad* (1999), authors Jacqueline Tobin and Raymond Dobard delineated the symbolism of quilt patterns once used to guide fugitives, according to the oral account of an African American woman basket maker in Charleston.[3] The presentation of secret knowledge hidden within quilt square diagrams captured the imaginations of readers, inspiring themed quilt pattern books, elementary school lesson plans, and colorful posters featuring the special patterns.[4] Runaway slaves, quilts, and a secret code was an intoxicating combination for public audiences who were fascinated by code breaking and adventure, the quilt historian Teri Klassen has explained.[5]

But those who embrace the inspiring idea of the handmade quilt serving as a tool of Black liberation need not fully give up on the notion. An account of Harriet Tubman's story that hews closely to existing evidence still bears witness to the role of the quilt in the quest for freedom. Although academic historians agree that no firm evidence exists to corroborate the existence of a widespread secret quilt code, the argument took hold.[6] Even today, references to the code regularly surface. Recent forums—a 2022 Museum of Fine Arts, Boston, panel on the quilt exhibition *Fabric of a Nation,* a discussion of the difficulty of escape on the now shuttered Black News Channel in 2022, and an essay on Harriet Tubman posted to Medium in 2020—have all referenced the secret quilt code as common knowledge.[7]

Harriet Tubman was a skilled quilter, as were many Black Southern women in the early and mid-nineteenth century. And a quilt would turn out to be one of her most crucial resources in the fall of 1849. As she stole away from Thompson's grounds, traveling mostly by night, she turned to people in the countryside who could offer her a place to hide, share provisions, or provide information. The first person to help, as far as the historical record reveals, was a white woman in the area who may have been a Quaker. Harriet disclosed her intentions and need of assistance to this woman, offering her a hand-pieced quilt in return. The woman, in turn, gave Harriet a valuable bit of intelligence. "Harriet had a bed quilt which she highly prized, a quilt she had pieced together," said Helen Tatlock, who knew Tubman later in New York.[8] "She gave this bed quilt to the white woman . . . The white woman gave her a paper with two names upon it, and directions how she might get to the first house."[9]

Just as Harriet's work in the woods revealed her outdoor

skills, this story about a crucial exchange shows that she practiced the craft of quilt-making and took pride in her handiwork. Harriet might not have wished to part with her "prized" quilt made of textures and colors we can see only in our imagination. Nevertheless, her ownership of the one-of-a-kind bed covering gave her leverage. She must have learned a memorable lesson in this moment: self-emancipation would have to be funded. In a manner less elaborate than the quilt-code notion would indicate, but far more instructive and replicable, Harriet used a textile to jump-start her solo journey. And according to one of her associates, Harriet worked quilts by hand while hiding in the woods during her subsequent rescue missions: "By day they lay in the woods; then she pulled out her patchwork, and sewed together little bits, perhaps not more than [sic] inch square, which were afterwards made into comforters for the fugitives in Canada."[10] The art and craft of quilt-making that channeled Black women's creative expression and provided enslaved and refugee families with cover and comfort also provided Black women with a trade good, a material form of currency, which underwrote the project of emancipation.[11]

With the information gained through this trade, Harriet found the safe house, the first in a series that would carry her across Maryland's countryside. Her exact route and helpers are unknown to this day. Tubman kept them safe and secret.

She probably made her way at first to a long-standing Quaker settlement in Caroline County, which was also home to a Black community. She may have been aided by the Levertons, a Quaker family in a neighboring area whom historians have documented as playing an active part in the secret network to aid fugitives in Maryland.[12]

Scholars speculate that Harriet likely followed a trail that many other fugitives from slavery had taken along the Choptank River (named for a local Indigenous nation), heading northeast toward the distant state border. In this way, she was again acting in a manner that fit within a larger, collective experience of enslaved people in the Upper South region of eastern Maryland. A contemporary biographer of Tubman, Catherine Clinton, sketched out that riverine route as one "which reaches far inland, cutting a swath across the verdant Delmarva peninsula (shared by western Delaware, eastern Maryland, and a small offshore slice of Virginia at the southern most point)." Another present-day biographer, Kate Larson, has detailed Tubman's most likely route as running from Preston to Sandtown to Camden to Dover, to Odessa to New Castle to Wilmington, and finally to Chester and Philadelphia. Harriet traveled mostly by night to avoid detection, knowing the horsemen of her visions must be in pursuit, entrusting her safety to individuals who could betray her at any moment, and relying on her past experience in wild and cultivated nature. "She later confided that she had observed that all streams she knew ran north to south," Clinton has noted. "So Tubman might have used the direction of flowing water as a guide during her first foray."[13]

Harriet believed that God guided and shielded her, a view she shared with other women of her faith tradition. Just as certainly, she was behaving in ways her family and local community members would have recognized and understood. Her father had taught her the ways of the forest. Her mother had fled to the woods to save her brother from sale. Hundreds of others in Maryland had attempted to flee chattel bondage over land and waterways in the year 1850 alone.[14] Harriet Tubman was a member of a regional and racial culture, not a lone ranger or solitary hero of the deep woods like the mythological figure, usually male, who pervades American and British lore.

The character Robin Hood epitomizes this traditional male Western hero. Robin Hood famously used the English forest as cover while stealing from the rich and giving to the poor in stories set in medieval times. Robin Hood's cultural mystique derives from fourteenth- and fifteenth-century England, when these oral stories centering him were first written down. The fictionalized Robin Hood represented a class of English noblemen pushed off their lands after William the Conqueror's Norman Conquest in 1066. These nobles turned to the forest, where they "continued to resist the invaders through guerilla warfare," the literature scholar Robert Pogue Harrison has explained. Their "reckless raids and reprisals . . . became the matter of legends and popular ballads, giving birth to a fabulous figure who would continue to fascinate the popular imagination for centuries to come: that of the heroic outlaw fighting the forces of injustice from his lair in the forest."[15] The Robin Hood character was beloved for his willingness to dwell beyond the bounds of settled society to make a political staging ground of the forest.

Black, female, family- and community-oriented, without any claim to noble birth—and a breathing, feeling person who surely cried and bled in those woods—Harriet Tubman was no Robin Hood. So who was her archetypal antecedent? What if we were to see Tubman's affect and actions as rooted in a tradition of the female fugitive passed down in story and art? This tradition, and the changeable figure at its center, is long-lived in the imaginations of Blacks in bondage and their descendants. The trope was perhaps most memorably expressed by the writer Alice Walker when she offered the following example to define her new term *womanism* in the 1980s: "Traditionally capable, as in: 'Mama, I'm walking to Canada and I'm taking you and a bunch of other slaves with me.' Reply: 'It wouldn't be the first time.'"[16]

Harriet Tubman was one of these traditionally capable

daughters who represented a spirit of undaunted human-ity. And beyond her Southern American roots, she stood in an even longer line of brave captive women dating back to ancient times. Did Harriet think of herself as a narrative descendant of Hagar, a biblical figure highlighted in Black Christian thought across generations? Hagar was sexually enslaved by Abraham, who could not bear children with his

Hagar. Edmonia Lewis sculpted this biblically inspired work out of white marble in 1875. The overturned jar at Hagar's feet is often interpreted as symbolizing the challenge of providing for her child while enslaved and outcast.

Smithsonian Institution, open access.

wife Sarah; she was then exiled into the wilderness after Sarah finally conceived. Wandering the open land with her child, Ishmael, son of Abraham, Hagar had to depend on God to survive. "God gave her [Hagar] a new vision to see survival resources where she had not seen them before," theologian Delores Williams has written. In the late nineteenth century, the Afro-Ojibwe sculptor Edmonia Lewis reflected this resonant cultural motif in her choice of subject matter, chiseling a statue of Hagar in marble that won her wide acclaim.[17]

Harriet, like Hagar, made her way through the wilderness, perhaps under the watchful eye of the Hebrews' God. The journey of nearly 150 miles would have taken approximately forty-nine hours on foot, without the conveniences of modern roads or the reassurances of drawn maps. Harriet surely felt heavy while placing one heel in front of the other, as if she were "draggin[g] the moon like a shackle."[18] But the woods, which changed their trees like dresses as Harriet trudged northward, were with her on this path into darkness. Oaks and chestnuts shedding their colors intermixed with the pines as she trudged through leaves and over rocks of the piedmont hills, finally reaching that geographical borderline long featured in her dreams.[19] When Harriet stepped or crawled onto the free soil of Pennsylvania after one to two weeks of grueling travel, she rejoiced in her spirit. And perhaps the spirits of the trees sang a song of gladness with her. According to Sarah Bradford's account, Harriet described her overwhelming feelings of relief and joy in language that reflected her love of the natural *and* supernatural worlds. "I looked at my hands . . . to see if I was the same person now I was free. There was such a glory over everything, the sun came like gold through the trees, over the fields, and I felt like I was in heaven."[20]

This expression of the sublime, a sense of awestruck intimacy with the divinity of life refracted through natural beauty and captured in words, is attributed to Tubman in the same cultural moment—the mid-nineteenth century—when literary giants like Ralph Waldo Emerson and Henry David Thoreau formed a philosophical and literary movement of spiritual naturalism that embraced the same mood. Tubman was a philosopher, too, interpreting her surroundings and striving to make meaning of what she observed and experienced. But for her, this transcendent moment was fleeting, immediately dissolving into despair. Her status as a Black captive woman born to an enslaved family compromised her experience of transcendence. "I had crossed the line of which I had so long been dreaming. I was free; but there was no one to welcome me to the land of freedom, I was a stranger in a strange land, and my home after all was down in the old cabin quarter, with the old folks, and my brothers and sisters; I was free, and they should be free," Harriet said.[21] Her recurring dream of the borderline had been realized in its deeper symbolic meanings. Just as her dream had foretold in its earliest iterations, she had come crashing down to earth. If slavery had been hell, she would now dwell in emotional purgatory, forbidden peace while her relatives suffered and the question still burned inside her: Would they ever be saved?

Somewhere on the slopes of southern Pennsylvania, Harriet Tubman was in crisis. She had found the promised land by the time morning dawned, but she was destined to enter it without the companionship of those she loved. Harriet Jacobs, who escaped her abusive owner in North Carolina in the 1840s, described her feelings upon reaching Philadelphia with another bondswoman: "Before us lay the city of strangers. We looked at each other, and the eyes of both were moistened with tears. We had escaped from slavery, and we supposed ourselves to be safe from the hunters. But we were alone in the world, and we had left dear ties behind us; ties cruelly sundered by the demon Slavery."[22] Harriet Tubman was similarly bereft. She felt achingly lonely, and certainly afraid—but that is not all. She felt aggrieved by a society and circumstance that would have her freed while her loved ones remained enchained by the demon. Her personal bereavement became a political realization about the unfair nature of power.

As we would expect, having followed Tubman from her childhood yearnings to her adulthood stirrings, she turned to God in her desolation, begging him to hear her appeal. "I would make a home for them in the North, and the Lord helping me, I would bring them all there. Oh, how I prayed then, lying all alone on the cold, damp ground; 'Oh, dear Lord . . . I haven't got no friend but you. Come to my help, Lord, for I'm in trouble!'"[23] Harriet believed what her cultural contemporary the preacher Elizabeth had learned as an enslaved child: there was no one to look to but God. On freedom's border, Harriet made a pact with herself and with a deity: she would become her own answer to her second existential question. There *would be* deliverance for her people. With God's aid, it was she who would rescue them. This was an oath drawn not in blood but in the rocky piedmont soil—the very ground that held her body, smelling of sweat and sweet decay like the cast-off leaves of autumn trees— as she whispered her petition. Nature bore witness to this epiphany wrapped inside an appeal, the moment when Harriet Tubman determined she would cross back into hell, "breath weak an[d] bone sore," to set her people free.[24]

Harriet rose from the ground, pulling the weight of survivor's guilt over her shoulders like a shawl. With this invisible burden dragging her down through the last, long miles, she finally made it to Philadelphia, where she knew not a single soul. Studded with densely packed, architecturally grand buildings and a large, bustling population, Philadelphia was the destination of many fugitives seeking safe harbor. The city had been the home of Quaker critics of the slave trade since the mid-1700s and a hotbed of abolitionist activity since the 1830s. Black and white activists operated in tandem from the city center, forming the Pennsylvania Anti-Slavery Society and organizing the Philadelphia Vigilant Committee to watch the streets for freedom seekers in need as well as for slave hunters on the prowl.[25] Black freedom activists Robert Purvis and William Still (born of formerly enslaved parents) were based in the city. The white Quaker activist Thomas Garrett moved between this urban hub and his home and shop in Delaware, where he and his wife, Rachel Mendenhall Garrett, housed runaways and provided them with clothing, shoes, food, and other supplies.[26]

But Harriet Tubman did not immediately find this circle of support. She was alone when she entered the gritty streets of the city, more bewildering to her, a rural newcomer, than the forested wilderness from which the term *bewildered* is derived. After days or weeks in the city, she may have met other Black women who offered aid, counsel, and company.

She managed to secure temporary work, "in hotels, in club houses, and afterwards at Cape May," a seaside resort town in nearby New Jersey, Sarah Bradford related.[27] Every day, Harriet must have felt the tenuousness and urgency of her situation. She had endured a terrifying trek on top of a traumatic childhood. She was in a big, new, disorienting place where she could not read street signs or newspapers. She suffered from headaches and seizures. But Harriet was not focused on her own emotional recovery or physical comfort. She had a mission that extended beyond herself. She aimed to help her relatives, and she knew from experience that escape from a Southern state even as far north as Maryland required resources, information, courage, and sacrifice. After two years spent "working in Philadelphia and carefully hoarding her money," reported Ednah Cheney, Harriet "hired a room, furnished it as well as she could, bought a nice suit of men's clothes, and went back to Maryland for her husband."[28]

But Ednah Cheney left something out, as Tubman's early biographers often did, or else Cheney was unaware of the first feat in what would become nearly a decade of astounding rescues that fellow activists would call "trips of mercy."[29] Harriet had maintained close personal connections with residents in Baltimore, and she heard through the grapevine that a young relation was in trouble. Before Harriet went back for her husband, she attempted to save her niece Kessiah, who was once again targeted by Eliza Brodess for the auction block. In December of 1850, news of the impending sale had traveled to Harriet by way of community connections reaching from rural Maryland to the urban zones of Baltimore and Philadelphia.[30] Fearing for Kessiah, Harriet sprang into action.

Kessiah then acted on a plan developed by her inventive aunt, making her way to Baltimore with children in tow, with the aid of her husband, a sailor. Kessiah rendezvoused with Harriet, who hid the family among associates in the city before guiding them to Philadelphia. It had required temerity and teamwork to bring this niece, the daughter of a sold-away sister, out of slavery. In the act of helping her niece, Harriet risked exposing herself in a worsening political environment. In September of 1850, the passage of the enhanced federal Fugitive Slave Law heightened the danger for every runaway who had escaped or planned to run to the North. They would now be subject to recapture by Northern state officials and citizens alike. In this frenzied period of intense fear when people who had formerly freed themselves began to uproot from Northern cities and head to Canada, Harriet went south, straight into the red zone. A few months after helping Kessiah, Harriet traveled to Baltimore again to aid in the escapes of her brother Moses (whom her mother, a role model, had once hidden in the woods) and two other

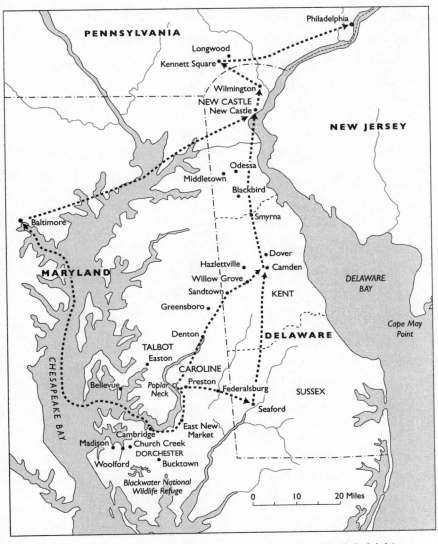

Harriet Tubman's southern Underground Railroad routes to Philadelphia.

Courtesy of Bill Nelson of Bill Nelson Maps and Kate Larson.

men. Only then, in the fall of 1851, two years after her own escape, did she make a move to reunite with her husband.[31]

Harriet still battled with chronic pain, sudden seizures, and disruptive visions. With limited energy, resources, and stamina, she had to choose each move she made with caution and care. Familial love and a triage mentality, which organized action in accordance with urgency, trumped romantic attachment in Harriet's decision-making process. But when she decided the time had come to bring her spouse (a free man) north to live with her, she was taking her greatest risk of recapture up to that point. She did not have an advance understanding with John Tubman. She would have to find him and convince him to leave all he knew behind. To do this, Harriet would have to push past the city of Baltimore, where she could more readily hide, and return to the rural Eastern Shore of her roots.

She must have been gravely afraid as she retraced her steps to the Land of Egypt where rewards had been promised to anyone who captured her.[32] And when she did find John, fear was soon flooded by an onrush of other emotions: misery, envy, resentment. For Harriet would learn that John had remarried in her absence, starting a new life with a Black woman who had possessed the one thing Harriet had lacked as a young person: freedom. It must have been a crushing blow, realizing someone she cared for enough to risk liberty had not cared enough in return to remain loyal to their relationship. "At first her grief and anger were excessive," Cheney wrote of Tubman. "She said 'she did not care what [master] did to her . . . she was determined to see her old man once more' . . . but finally she thought . . . 'if he could do without her, she could do without him,' and so 'he dropped out of her heart.'"[33]

It is difficult to believe that Harriet could so quickly rebound from the pain of this betrayal and the knowledge that her marriage was dead. Surely, she mourned her first love and whatever dream of a life with John Tubman she had harbored over the lonely months of their separation. Surely, too, she bore a heart wound as she backed away from the meeting place where she spoke—heatedly, desperately, tearfully?—with the man whose name she had once proudly taken. Nevertheless, she chose to pivot, accepting the loss of a marriage and focusing on what this transformed moment called for. She would not waste this costly voyage. She determined what must be done next. She regrouped, gathered a party of those more willing than her spouse, and led them to freedom in Philadelphia.

Harriet Tubman had wanted to stay married to John Tubman. That much is clear from her actions. But in losing this man, and whatever hope she may have placed in raising children with him in the future, she gained fresh possibilities. If she had lived with a husband in the same household or had young ones to care for in what would turn out to be a critical decade, the 1850s, when the nation was hurtling toward heated debate about the expansion of slavery that would soon culminate in civil war, Harriet's future would have unfolded differently. She might have been overtaken by domestic and parental duties, affording her less time and energy to attend to the work of rescue. Her singleness in this period, then, was essential to her autonomy, her flexibility, and her increased tolerance for risk. And Tubman shared singleness with other women of her faith culture who found that they had to first challenge male authority in their homes and churches before stepping out to preach God's word.

Elizabeth, who was "strengthened by the Lord's power, to go on to the fulfillment of His work" in midlife, had never married, according to her memoir, which meant she was always free from the demands and encumbrances of wedlock and domestic life. Jarena Lee's evangelical work flourished only after the death of her husband. In her memoir, Jarena calls this death "the greatest affliction of all" but also attributes it to "his [God's] hand." After her husband's passing, Jarena became a widow, "with no other dependence than the promise of Him," as she cared for two small children. She wrote that God "raised [her] up friends" to support her. And only after the loss of her husband did Jarena experience a significant life turn, with her "call to preach renewed."[34]

Zilpha Elaw also suffered the death of her spouse, in 1823, writing that "God was [her] strong tower and [her] refuge in the day of distress." Financially devastated due to the loss of her husband's income, Zilpha placed her daughter and herself in household servant positions, struggling for two years until she prayed for a "token" from God to affirm her "call to the ministry." Perceiving that this requested sign had been bestowed, she left her daughter in the care of "a dear relative" and relocated to Philadelphia to "commence" her "Master's business." She traveled alone from Pennsylvania to New York and preached there for seven months while "the Lord rendered [her] ministry a blessing to many souls." In 1828, Zilpha traveled south to preach, "regardless," writes the literary scholar William Andrews, "of the very real danger of being arrested or kidnapped and sold as a slave." Toward the end of her career, in 1840, Zilpha Elaw spent five years ministering in London and various English towns, "exhibiting," she wrote, "as did the bride of Solomon, comeliness with blackness." In other words, Black was beautiful in the scripture as Zilpha interpreted it. From beginning to end in her spiritual memoir, Zilpha Elaw articulated a race and gender analysis that exposed the degree of hardship she faced due to her identity, as well as her ultimate triumph as a Black woman under God's sponsorship.[35]

Julia Foote's break from the husband who deemed her "crazy" was more radical than that of the other evangelizing women described here. When her husband ordered her to cease her fervent religious expressions, threatening to return her to her parents, he was met with flagrant disobedience. Julia increased her spiritual activities, alienating her spouse in what became an emotional and physical, if not legal, separation. She attended an African Methodist Episcopal Conference in Philadelphia on her own, and there found community with three other women who felt called to preach but were stymied by male leadership. Julia rented space to hold prayer meetings in the city and then went west. In the 1840s she preached in upstate New York, Pittsburgh, Cincinnati, Columbus, and Cleveland, pausing to care for her ailing father in between. In 1850 she preached across the Ohio countryside, in Detroit, and over the border in Canada. Julia urged other women to follow their hearts, saying: "Sisters, shall not you and I unite with the heavenly host in the grand chorus? If so, you will not let what man may say or do, keep you from doing the will of the Lord or using the gifts you have for the good of others. How much easier to bear the reproach of men than to live at a distance from God."[36]

As widows, singles through separation, or never married "spinsters," these Black holy women could make decisions with greater independence from human male authority—Black or white. They could travel, speak their minds, lead prayers, and offer exhortations, pursuing what they all described as a divine calling. Freed from wedlock though not by choice, Harriet Tubman used her unexpected autonomy to fulfill what she conceived as her purpose. She, too, had heard God's voice and felt called to evangelize. Hers was a message of freedom, at once religious, social, and political—embedded in and expressed through her rescue work. In the early 1850s, when Julia Foote was preaching the gospel in the Midwest and Upper Canada (today's Ontario), defying her husband in the process, Harriet Tubman was preaching the gospel in the Southern woods and salted swamps, having left her first marriage behind in the dust of memory.

Harriet's message was not precisely the same as other Black holy women of her time who focused primarily on spiritual liberation, nor was it one that she had simply received from God whole cloth. Instead, Harriet's creed of holistic freedom was one that she had negotiated, or co-created through communion, with this god of her belief. She had formed a compact with God that grew stronger and more refined as she matured. The first draft of this compact seems to have been forged when she prayed for her owner to die and then begged forgiveness when he did, asking God to cleanse her soul. Then she learned not only that God sided with the oppressed but also that God would respond when she spoke to him, and so she must calibrate her petitions. Harriet's divine compact had solidified at the inaugural crossing of the northern border where she informed her deity that she intended to rescue others with his help.

Harriet believed God championed freedom. She had seen evidence of it. But she also urged him to support her as she broadened this vision beyond her own welfare. Her mission was not to liberate herself alone, or even to save individual souls or individual bodies from sin like other Black holy women were passionately doing, but instead to release a composite body, those whom she called "her people," from the evil grasp of the demon Slavery. "I have heard their groans and sighs, and seen their tears, and I would give every drop of blood in my veins to free them," she said.[37] Saving others was Harriet Tubman's grand idea, grounded in her own experience and her understanding of God's stance as revealed in the Old Testament stories, the death of her owner, and the success of her escape. She laid this freedom mission at the feet of her god, following and leading him at the same time.

Beginning with the redemption of her niece, Harriet

Tubman launched a series of incredible rescues. In the mid-1850s, as her liberation mission concretized and she found through experience that God was holding up his end, she acted with greater confidence, believing she understood the duties of each party in the compact. She would do God's will in freeing the people, and God would be there to guide and protect her. She developed a general route, "by way of Poplar Neck, Cambridge, where her father and mother were, and Baltimore, where her cousin Tom was," Tubman would later tell late-nineteenth-century Underground Railroad historian Wilbur Siebert. And she had by then joined the tight-knit network of regional activists, relying on Thomas Garrett (in Wilmington, Delaware) for material aid and on William Still (in Philadelphia) for critical information and communications. She gained renown among her colleagues as a "sister of humanity," and a "shrewd and fearless agent" who "well understood the entire route from that part of the country to Canada." Even as, by 1857, Thomas Garrett wrote, "I think there will be more danger at present than heretofore," Harriet Tubman pressed her purpose. She forged ahead with "utter disregard of consequences," as William Still put it. Sarah Bradford reported about Tubman's risky missions and near-miss escapes from recapture: "But these sudden deliverances never seemed to strike her as at all strange or mysterious; her prayer was the prayer of faith, and she *expected* an answer."[38]

Harriet's radical acts of rescue under the wing of divine providence were forms of preaching. She taught as she did, setting an example of faith and follow-through for others around her. She also used direct speech to exhort her listeners—freedom seekers—toward a clearer and deeper understanding of her religious message. Her songs (mostly hymns) and sayings (often repeated) functioned as micro sermons or homilies. As she accompanied people fortunate enough to leave their captors, she sang to pass on information, to soothe nerves, and to share her liberation ethos. In one example, when she sought to lift the flagging spirits of a fugitive named Joe who was terrified that he would be caught and returned to bondage, Harriet preached: "The Lord had been with them in six troubles, and he would not desert them in the seventh." And when Harriet, Joe, and a tired band of runaways stood before a bridge in Niagara, New York, which they still had to cross before reaching Canada, she led a song that conveyed her religious belief: "Oh righteous Father, wilt thou not pity me, and help me on to Canada, where all the slaves are free." Once the danger had passed and the party stood on Canadian soil, Joe responded with a song of his own: "Glory to God and Jesus too, One more soul got safe; Oh, go and carry the news, One more soul got safe."[39] This

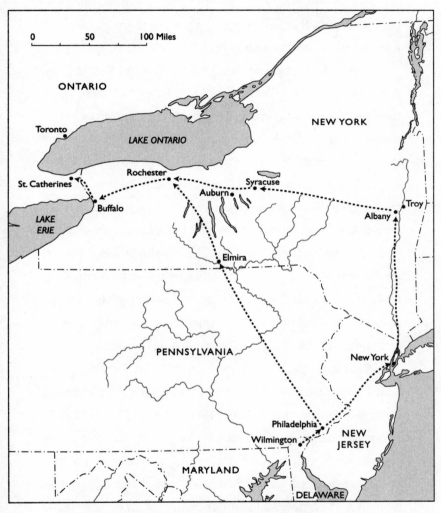

Harriet Tubman's northern Underground Railroad routes from
Philadelphia to St. Catharines, Canada.

Courtesy of Bill Nelson of Bill Nelson Maps and Kate Larson.

call and response between Harriet and one of her "passengers," set to rhythm before a group of self-emancipators, was a church service in transit.

In another instance when Harriet was guiding "a large party," including infants drugged with laudanum to quiet their crying, she would also turn to a hymn to convey information and religious conviction. Harriet had just thrown their pursuers off track and was hiding her group in the forest as darkness fell. Writes Bradford about this rescue: "All the others were on the alert, each one hidden behind his own tree, and silent as death. They had been long without food, and were nearly famished." Harriet left the group to search for nourishment, equipped as a forager who had learned the ways of the woods from her father and perhaps others in her community. Upon her return hours later, she sang a song to alert her party that it was safe to come out of hiding.

What must these frightened people have felt when they heard her voice rise through the trees, barely making out these words over the sound of their own rough heartbeats: "Around Him are ten thousand angels, Always ready to obey command; They are always hovering round you, Till you reach the heavenly land."[40] Harriet told them angels were near and they were safe in the hands of God. Harriet—a small, dark woman who might collapse at any moment—told these people remarkable things that belied perceptual reality. And despite the inconclusive nature of the message, the desolation of their location, and the evident physical ailments of their guide, they must have believed her, or wanted to. Although Harriet "half of her time . . . had the appearance of sleep, sit[ting] down by the road-side and go[ing] fast asleep when on her errands of mercy through the South," William Still said, "her followers generally had full faith in her."[41] And this stands to reason, for did not the very contrast between messenger and message prove God's power? Harriet Tubman as God's avenger bore certain similarities to the Bible stories the fugitives would have known well—of Moses cast away as a babe on the Nile in a basket, of Jesus born to an unwed teen beneath a star in a manger. Harriet's apparent weaknesses thrummed in tune with narrative chords of the Bible. So perhaps these were not weaknesses at all, her companions may have supposed, but rather, signs of holiness— or chosen-ness. After all, God could uplift the weak and imbue them with secret strengths, and often did the very same in the scriptures.

Early biographies of Tubman, as well as testimonials by people who knew her (and even the 2019 Hollywood biopic, *Harriet*), depict these years of the 1850s as a montage of near miracles. It is hard to resist this impulse and difficult to believe all that Harriet Tubman accomplished as the captain of her own freedom enterprise. Against all odds and in the face of recapture, resale, torture, and death, she rescued approximately seventy individuals from captivity, multiplied by the number of children they would birth and raise in freedom. This meant traveling north to south then back again time after time, when each trip presented a threat to her life and the lives of her companions. As a female who outpaced

Harriet Tubman around midlife, wearing a long skirt and delicate blouse with ruffles on the sleeves and cuff. Photo by Benjamin F. Powelson in his studio in Auburn, New York, circa 1867–69. "Harriet Tubman" is handwritten across the bottom of the photograph.

Library of Congress and the Smithsonian National Museum of African American History and Culture, public domain.

every single male conductor working on the Underground Railroad by leaps and bounds, she confronted the particularly grave danger of sexualized bodily harm. How could Harriet accept this risk once, twice, a dozen times? Who among us could imagine making such a perilous choice?[42]

Fortified in both mind and spirit by the conviction that moral duty superseded personal safety, Harriet Tubman applied practical knowledge to her missions. She had learned effective techniques from her own escape. She knew that season, weather, time of day, resources (financial and material), information, and networks of support were crucial to outcomes. Based on this experiential knowledge, she began a pattern of traveling south in cool weather—fall, winter, or early spring before the thaw—and returning north with groups seeking freedom. In the warmer months, she undertook paid domestic work to earn money for the cold-weather operations. After the implementation of the draconian Fugitive Slave Law, she began guiding travelers from Maryland directly to Ontario. "I wouldn't trust Uncle Sam with my people no longer," she said. "I brought them all clear off to Canada."[43]

The parties Tubman guided were large and small. She seems to have sheltered a group of eleven in the New York home of Frederick Douglass, a fellow abolitionist who had freed himself from bondage in Maryland. In 1858, Douglass wrote in a letter to antislavery advocates, withholding names for the sake of security: "One coloured woman, who escaped from Slavery eight years ago, has made several returns at great risk, and has brought out, since obtaining her freedom, fifty others from the house of bondage." As individuals got word of others' plans to escape with Tubman, they sometimes broke out on their own to join in. "Every time she went," Ednah Cheney wrote, "the dangers increased."[44]

Within a few years of her escape and as she successfully aided others, Harriet caught the attention of abolitionist activists in Philadelphia. It was only at this point, after she had undertaken and funded perhaps a handful of solo trips working with Baltimore contacts, that she was able to gather financial resources from other sources beyond her own domestic labor. Thomas Garrett, upon learning of her exploits from Philadelphia colleagues, befriended Tubman and began to collect funds for her missions. Each time she stopped by his place in Delaware, she retrieved a new pair of shoes, basic but essential items for her endeavors.[45]

But Harriet had not yet rescued all her family members, so she kept on going back. In 1854, after sensing that her brothers were in trouble, she dictated brilliantly coded letters to them through a free Black associate. She orchestrated an escape for three of them, Ben, Robert, and Henry, arriving at her old stomping grounds on Christmas Eve, "a Saturday, the perfect timing for an escape," the historian Kate Larson has said, as enslavers often allowed Black workers more flexibility of movement during the holidays.[46] All four siblings (and Jane, Ben's fiancée, who had just escaped a violent owner, disguised as a man) stopped by their parents' cabin in Poplar Neck near the Choptank River before departing. They kept out of view of their mother, Rit, while catching the attention of their father, Ben. A clever man, Ben Ross blindfolded himself so he could swear to anyone who might later interrogate him that he had not "seen" his children. He gave them food and allowed them to hide in his corncrib, then walked arm in arm with them, eyes still covered, until they parted ways.[47]

Harriet was gaining a reputation for bravery, reliability, and perhaps for revealing a glint of God's favor. "By reason of her frequent visits there, always carrying away some of the oppressed, she got among her people the name of 'Moses,' which she still retains," Sarah Bradford proclaimed.[48] But even as Harriet was earning that byname and the mystique that clouds our view of her now, she did face failure. She tried but did not succeed in bringing her sister (probably Rachel) and her sister's children out of slavery during the Christmas rescue of 1854.[49] The haunting scene in her memory of sisters sold away would never fade. Neither the ones who had been lost nor the lone sister still on the Eastern Shore would be redeemed by "Moses," their wrongs avenged and their honor restored.

In 1857, Harriet returned to Maryland for the parents who had trained her so well for survival. Although Ben and Rit were both free by then—Ben through his owner's will and Rit through Ben's purchase of her—they remained under threat as long as they lived in the South. Ben had become active on the Underground Railroad, and he was targeted for arrest after helping someone escape. He could be jailed, beaten, or worse. Harriet, a "conductor" then in that same loose network of operators, was determined to bring him out. She arrived, as was her custom, in the dark, equipped with the tools necessary to transport her elderly parents. Did Ben Ross proudly think "Like father like daughter" when he saw the makeshift wooden conveyance, a rudimentary wagon, that she had procured to ease their travel? Did he think of the times he had taught her to move heavy logs out of the woods? Did Rit Green find that Harriet had packed pieced quilts into the vehicle, sewn by her own hand with skills learned at Rit's knee in childhood?

Harriet established a household for her parents in St. Catharines, Ontario, a town that would become a second home to her in this period. And although that first winter was hard on her parents, who missed the temperate Southern climate, Harriet had no regrets. "Now I've been free," she said in an interview in Canada a year before bringing her parents there, "I know what a dreadful condition slavery is. I have seen hundreds of escaped slaves, but I never saw one who was willing to go back and be a slave."[50]

Maryland enslavers and slave hunters placed bounties on Harriet's head. The first advertisement for her recapture, before she had become infamous for aiding others in their escapes, offered a reward of $50 or $100, depending on whether she was caught inside or outside of Maryland. By the end of the 1850s, she had undertaken nearly thirteen trips in all and freed seventy to eighty people, undercutting the property values of enslavers like the Brodesses and the Thompsons.[51] Nineteenth-century primary accounts and early-twentieth-century commentary give different figures for the bounty, which may have been exaggerated. Sarah Bradford mentions $12,000 (without documentation), and W. E. B. Du Bois claimed $10,000 (perhaps drawing from Bradford).[52] Whatever the exact figure, Harriet was a wanted woman. But "[f]earlessly she went on," Sarah Bradford opined, "trusting in the Lord." Bradford offered a statement of Tubman's logic in her rendition of Tubman's words: "There's *two* things I've got a *right* to, and these are, Death or Liberty—one or the other I mean to have. No one will take me back alive; I shall fight for my liberty, and when the time has come for me to go, the Lord will let them kill me."[53]

Bradford summarized this statement as "a simple creed." We can instead see it is a complex philosophy emerging from Tubman's religious belief, moral reasoning, and lived experience.

Harriet believed she had divinely endowed rights, even as a Black-slave-woman, a recombinant mix of the lowest categories in American, and indeed global, society. Her understanding of these rights was rooted in her religious faith in which God championed liberation and was no respecter of persons. It was also based (if Bradford's quotation fairly approximates Tubman's words) in the language of natural rights (now understood as human rights) embedded in the founding documents of the United States. The will of God, as well as the letter of the moral law guiding the nation into which she was born a chattel-child, authorized her action. There were no higher powers in this land, and Harriet Tubman knew it. With God on her side, in a country that espoused self-evident truths of human worth as endowed by God, she believed she would prevail. And she did.

Harriet trusted that God was with her, personally and politically. This is a through line across her life story. From a young age, through ritual and repetition within a shared religious frame, Harriet had come to feel God was real, present, and responsive. She was in the habit of walking and talking with this invisible being. Her comrade Thomas Garrett wrote in a testimonial: "She has frequently told me that she talked with God, and he talked with her every day of her life, and she has declared to me that she felt no more fear of being arrested by her former master, or any other person, when in his immediate neighborhood, than she did in the State of New York, or Canada, for she said she never ventured only where God sent her, and her faith in a Supreme Power truly was great."[54] People who conversed with Harriet said she credited God as her key informant and the impetus behind her decisions, often saying "The Lord told me." Once Thomas Garrett pressed Harriet on an occasion when she had come to visit, saying God told her Garrett had money for her next rescue. He asked whether "God never deceived her?" because he had received no such funds. Tubman proclaimed, "No!" And according to Garrett, the mystery cash soon arrived.[55] In 1860, when Garrett worried in a letter to William Still about Tubman's latest trip with two families, he commented: "I shall be very uneasy about them until I hear they are safe. There is much more risk on the road . . . yet, as it is Harriet who seems to have had a special angel to guard her on her journey of mercy, I have hope."[56]

Harriet's faith in her compact with God, poetically reflected in her movement name, Moses, permeates nineteenth-century accounts of her life. Years after her breathtaking rescues, Harriet described numerous occasions when she was nearly discovered, and her fellow travelers almost re-captured. Once while traveling through a Maryland village, she saw a man who had previously rented her. She quickly devised a ruse to hide in plain sight. Not for the first time in her life, she relied on farm animals for cover. In the village market, she bought two chickens and a bonnet. She placed the hat on her head to shadow her features and tied the legs of the chickens together. When she saw this former "master" approaching, she untied the birds and "pinched them poor chickens until they squawked and fluttered like they were going to get away from me." As she stooped over to gather her fowls as if in a panic, she watched the man walk past her "never susp[ecting] that it was Mrs. Harriet he wanted so bad that was right there under his eyes." On another occasion, while on a train, she saw a former "master," grabbed a discarded newspaper, and held it in front of her face. She knew that he knew she "couldn't read" and therefore would not suspect her.[57]

During a trip launched to help an enslaved woman named Tilly escape to join with her fiancé, who had self-emancipated to Canada, Harriet traveled south to Baltimore. Harriet located Tilly in accordance with the plan orchestrated with the fiancé. But without free papers for the young woman (Harriet herself had counterfeit papers produced in advance by a Philadelphia steamboat captain), the pair would be suspect if they attempted to go north by boat. Harriet convinced a captain in Baltimore to manufacture a travel pass or certificate for Tilly. The women then steamed in a southerly direction to avoid suspicion, with the intention of circling back the next day. Harriet talked their way into a hotel room and meal for the night in the town of Seaford, Delaware, south of Baltimore, but morning brought fresh danger. A slave dealer noticed the two Black women traveling alone and threatened to arrest them. Tilly's panic mounted during this risk-filled delay, which increased their degree of exposure. Harriet's response was to make an appeal to her god, praying then as she most likely had throughout the night. "Having no other help," Sarah Bradford wrote, Harriet prayed: "Oh, Lord! You've been with me in six troubles, don't *desert* me in the seventh!" As Tilly's fear visibly spiked, Harriet repeated the line. "You've been with me in six troubles!" She flashed Tilly's travel pass in lieu of free papers and, with that move, secured their safe passage. They were able to board a ship and steam away unmolested.[58]

In another deus ex machina story from the early accounts, Harriet was leading a group when she suddenly changed course after receiving a message from God. The sun had risen while the group trudged onward. In daylight, they were more vulnerable to exposure. Bradford recounted that Harriet "stood one moment in the street, and in that moment she had flashed a message quicker than that of the telegraph to her unseen Protector, and the answer came as quickly; in a suggestion to her of an almost forgotten place of refuge." Harriet remembered that outside of town lay a swampy island. She led the group there and "waded into the swamp, carrying in a basket two well-drugged babies (these were a pair of little twins)." The party remained hidden for hours, suffering from cold, damp, and hunger. "Harriet's faith never wavered, her silent prayer still ascended, and she confidently expected help," Bradford reported. Just after dusk, a Quaker approached the edge of the swamp and whispered the location of his wagon.[59]

In yet another example of a seemingly inexplicable series of events, Emma Telford recounts an incident originally described by Thomas Garrett. Here, Harriet was leading "a large party of men" alongside a "deep stream" when she "stopped short saying, 'Children, we must stop here and cross this here river.'" The men hesitated, frightened by the rushing water. Harriet, in her Moses-parting-the-Red-Sea moment that has gone down in history, waded into the water. "It was cold, in the month of March, but Harriet having confidence in her guide went into the water, it came up to her arm pits; the men refused to follow till they saw her safe on the opposite shore," Garrett related. "They then followed, and if I mistake not she had soon to wade a second stream!"[60]

In Sarah Bradford's chronicle of this event, Harriet had "received one of her sudden intimations that danger was ahead." She quotes Tubman as saying: "The water never came above my chin; when we thought we were all going under, it became shallower and shallower, and we came out safe on the other side."[61]

Harriet Tubman attributed moments like these to divine intervention. They were cases of "the Lord sav[ing]" her, she said.[62] She told Bradford and others who expressed surprise at these feats: "It wasn't me, it was the Lord! Just so long as he wanted to use me, he would take care of me, and when he didn't want me no longer, I was ready to go; I always told him, I'm going to hold steady on to you, and you've got to see me through."[63] According to Emma Telford, Tubman "always escaped by her quick wit or as she calls it 'warnings from heaven.'" These warnings seem to have been intuitions, flickers of awareness, or quicksilver syntheses of subconscious observations that Harriet experienced as God-given. "'When danger is near . . . [it] appears like my heart goes flutter, Flutter! And then they may say 'peace, peace! As much as they like, I know it's going to be war!!'" Harriet said, as quoted by Telford.[64]

Harriet may have believed she possessed what Telford called "the gift of foresight." Apparently, Harriet told others that this was so. It is also certainly true that she was taking in her surrounds, calling to mind things she knew, and thinking about those data points. In the rising river story, she would certainly have used her five senses to gauge that waterway, perhaps considering the water level and speed of flow, and only then deciding that wading in was relatively safe. She could have run this analysis while in the midst of praying, as prayer was, as we have touched on previously, a form of thought as well as a spiritual practice. In the incident with Tilly, Harriet may have been evaluating the facial expressions and body language of the clerk, processing how he might behave and calculating how she might respond even as she stared at the water and prayed that God would save them. On the sunlit road when she suddenly changed course, she may have heard hunters on their heels without realizing the sensory source of the input, tapped into her mental map of the area, and recalled the location of the swamp island. The retrieval of this place memory might have been spurred by the reflective mental work of praying. While it can hardly be argued that Harriet conjured the Quaker wagon-owner with the powers of her mind, it is likely that her knowledge of local geography, rational evaluation of risks, and application of a strong skill set placed her and the people she guided within reach of his aid. Harriet may have operated with God's help, but she also helped God along with the talents she brought to bear.

Whatever the source of her special knowledge, super-natural, natural, or some inexpressible combination of both, Harriet's awareness of what was occurring in real time around her and also of what might happen next based on human nature and environmental context seems even now preternatural, or beyond the normal course of things. She had a gift for scanning natural and social environments, projecting and assessing potential scenarios, calculating risk, and forming blisteringly quick plans that she then carried out with staggering confidence. Emma Telford was convinced of Harriet Tubman's unusual abilities: "Many and wonderful indeed are the instances known personally to the writer where Harriet [sic] predictions' [sic] of impending danger or her forecast of other events concerning which she could have had no possible information have been literally fulfilled."[65]

Minty Ross had once been a powerless girl whose family members disappeared around her. Harriet Tubman was now an empowered woman concocting her own disappearing acts. The source of her power was fervent belief yoked to knowledge. Wrote Sarah Bradford about the havoc Harriet wreaked on the Eastern Shore: "The mysterious woman appeared—the woman on whom no one could lay his finger—and men, women, and children began to disappear from the plantations . . . before their masters were awake to the fact, the party of fugitives, following their intrepid leader, were far on their way towards liberty."[66]

To *Tubman's Way*, outlined in the introduction of this book as a path of spiritual, political, philosophical, and ecological belief, we can now add *Tubman's Tool Kit*. Harriet relied on God first and foremost. But she also needed concrete things in the material world to advance her mission: reliable information, social connections, money and materials, practical skills, geographical awareness, and environmental consciousness. She preferred to move in winter months, "when the nights are long and dark, and people who have homes stay in them," Ednah Cheney said. "She resorted to various devices," Cheney continued. "She had confidential friends all along the road. She would hire a man to follow the one who put up the notices [for escaped slaves], and take them down as soon as his back was turned. She crossed creeks on railroad bridges by night, she hid her company in the woods while she herself not being advertised went into the towns in search of information. If met on the road, her face was always to the south . . . She would get into the cars near her pursuers, and manage to hear their plans."[67]

Harriet's feats inspire awe, but there is always a cost to heroism. She believed in her system, her tools, and her god so much that she wagered well-being. She routinely ran the risk of hurting herself and others, and sometimes risk led to mishap and hardship. She directed mothers to drug their babies with an opium-based substance that could have caused overdose and death. She carried a revolver and did not hesitate to use it to threaten already traumatized people. Runaways who grew afraid and tried to turn back might face the barrel of her gun or the weapons of men she directed. Bradford summarized: "Sometimes members of her party would become exhausted, foot-sore, and bleeding, and declare they could not go on, they must stay where they dropped down, and die; others would think a voluntary return to slavery better than being overtaken and carried back, and would insist upon returning; then there was no remedy but force."[68] Harriet was willing to take a life, even one she was trying to save, rather than risk exposure of the whole group should a returnee betray them.

And she was just as harsh and unforgiving toward herself. She ran her body into the ground, working relentlessly to earn funds for the missions, taking on hundred-plus-mile journeys on foot, by rail, and by boat. She exposed herself to dangerous weather—beating rain and pelting snow. She submerged herself in chilled waters and submitted herself to cold winds. After that especially difficult trip when Harriet waded through waterways in the chill of March, she reemerged from the field with a raging toothache, an infection, surely, that she had suffered for days. And this pain would have been borne amid, or on top of, or behind—depending on how she experienced the sensation of chronic pain—her spontaneous headaches and seizures. Thomas Garrett saw her after this ordeal and described her condition. Harriet had found the fugitive group a place to stay overnight "in the cabin of colored people, who took them all in, put them to bed, and dried their clothes." This generous host family would also have been in need since poverty was the norm for Black households. Harriet intended, as was her custom, to offer a material trade for the help. But, Garrett related, "Harriet had run out of money, and gave them some of her under-clothing to pay for their kindness. When she called on me two days after, she was so hoarse she could hardly speak, and was also suffering with violent toothache."[69] Garrett continued with his chronicle of this rescue, pointing out the "strange part of the story," being that the owners of the fugitive men had been posting advertisements for their capture at the closest rail station, near enough to catch them had Harriet not veered into the stream. But we should pause a beat earlier, where we sense the price Harriet paid as she carried on without a warm layer of undergarments, having lost her voice due to sickness, and enduring invisible pain.

If Harriet found an evergreen tree to lean against on one of these final trips, sheltering there through a winter storm, as the story goes, she had become that tree by the time she was a veteran rescuer. The tree was a mirror of herself. Harriet's strength of body and mind, her vibrancy of spirit and faith, had formed a sturdy shelter for others, which meant it was she who bore the brunt of many storms, physically, psychologically, and emotionally. In the Bible, we might recall, Moses paid a high price for his burden of leadership over the long run. He disappointed God, who loved him nonetheless, and died with only a glimpse of the promised land. Harriet Tubman seems to have felt that her life was also dispensable. She was a willing martyr. "When the time has come for me to go, the Lord will let them kill me," she said.

6

THE DELIVERER

Go down Moses
Way down in Egypt land
Tell old Pharaoh to
Let My People Go!

—"GO DOWN MOSES,"

TRADITIONAL SPIRITUAL

She is well known to many by the various names which her eventful life has given her:

Harriet Garrison, Gen. Tubman, &c.; but among the slaves she is universally known by her well-earned title of Moses,—Moses the deliverer.

—EDNAH DOW CHENEY, "MOSES," 1865

Delivery is an art form. Harriet must have recognized this as she delivered time and again on her promise to free the people. Plying the woods and byways, she pretended to be someone she was not when she encountered enslavers or hired henchmen—an owner of chickens, or a reader, or an elderly woman with a curved spine, or a servile sort who agreed that her life should be lived in captivity. Each interaction in which Harriet convinced an enemy that she was who they believed her to be—a Black person properly stuck in their place—she was acting. Performance—gauging what an audience might want and how she might deliver it—became key to Harriet Tubman's tool kit in the late 1850s and early 1860s. In this period, when she had not only to mislead slave catchers but also to convince enslaved people to trust her with their lives, and antislavery donors to trust her with their funds, Tubman polished her skills as an actor and a storyteller. Many of the accounts that we now have of Tubman's most eventful moments were told by Tubman to eager listeners who wrote things down with greater or lesser accuracy. In telling these listeners certain things in particular ways, Tubman always had an agenda, or more accurately, multiple agendas that were at times in competition. She wanted to inspire hearers to donate cash or goods to the cause. She wanted to buck up the courage of fellow freedom fighters. She wanted to convey her belief that God was the engine behind her actions. And in her older age, in the late 1860s through the 1880s, she wanted to raise money to purchase and secure a haven for those in need.

There also must have been creative and egoistic desires mixed in with Harriet's motives. She wanted to be the one to tell her own story. She wanted recognition for her accomplishments even as she attributed them to God. She wanted to control the narrative that was already in formation about her life by the end of the 1850s. And she wanted to be a free agent in word as well as deed. To accomplish all these goals, a mature Tubman, then in her late thirties and forties, began to mount spoken word performances of her missions, merging storytelling with fundraising. These performances could be improvisational, taking shape in an instant when someone presented a question or a challenge, like the woman who asked about the storm that opens this book. Or these performances could be prepared affairs when she spoke to advocates in New England parlors or to interviewers on New York porches. Jean Humez, a Tubman scholar and literary critic, has succinctly summed up this aspect of Tubman's personality and biography, calling the activist a "life-storyteller."[1] Tubman "told stories, sang songs, and performed dramatic reenactments of many of the life experiences she considered most important," Humez has explained. "She was clearly an active participant in the creation of the public Harriet Tubman story."[2] Tubman wanted to learn to write so that she would gain even more control, but she was not able to set aside time to acquire the skill. She turned instead to dictation, preferring to touch the writer who put her ideas on the page, perhaps believing, as one such author put it, "that by laying her hand on this person, her feelings may be transmitted."[3] Tubman also relied on the oral intellectual and artistic culture in which she was raised, the culture of enslaved Black people who might not be able to read the Bible but breathed life into text with the spoken word.

As Harriet repeated these performances, she was shaping the characterization of herself as a "celebrated antislavery heroine," understanding that if she did not, others would make a character of her for their own ends.[4] In crafting stories that she thought would be most true to her self-concept and most effective for her cause, Harriet had a sense of what she was up against. Soon after her initial escape to Philadelphia, she became aware of a stage performance of Harriet Beecher Stowe's bestselling novel, *Uncle Tom's Cabin*. When her fellow domestic workers suggested that they view the play together, Harriet protested the prurient nature of the entertainment. "No," she said, "I ain't got no heart to go and see the sufferings of my people played on the stage. I've heard 'Uncle Tom's Cabin' read, and I tell you Mrs. Stowe's pen hasn't begun to paint what slavery is as I have seen it at the far South. I've seen *the real thing*, and I don't want to see it on no stage or in no theater."[5] Harriet assessed abolitionist art with the keen eye of a cultural critic, observing that slavery could be represented as melodrama and that enslaved people, like the protagonist of Stowe's story, Tom, could be portrayed in unrealistic, idealistic ways that diminished their dignity. As a teller of her own tale, she would walk a tightrope between giving listeners what they expected and what she felt they needed to know, between disclosing dramatic episodes and protecting secret routes, as well as her own private feelings. The texts that come down to us from eager listeners of Tubman's tales are complicated narratives produced out of this context of give-and-take in which the teller and the told had different desires.

Harriet Tubman had begun to narrate her own escape and freedom missions as early as 1854, when she told William Still the story of rescuing her three brothers. Still's office had become an information station for fugitives entering the city. He took copious secret notes on his work and later published an account titled *The Underground Railroad*. The Christmas Eve rescue and Ben Ross's blindfold trick entered the historical record when Tubman told it to Still, who wrote it down. Once she was introduced by word of mouth to Northeastern antislavery circles by other activists and advocates, including Frederick Douglass, who in 1858 described her as a person who "possesses great courage and shrewdness, and may yet render even more important service to the Cause," Tubman gained acclaim.[6] Interspersed with her last rescue missions and meetings with the abolitionist radical John Brown, Harriet followed a fundraising circuit. She visited Thomas Garrett to collect donations that were mailed to him from afar. She presented her story to small circles in private homes. The greater Boston area, an abolitionist hub equal in organizational strength to Philadelphia and New York City, became a fount for Harriet's fundraising. She made friends who had still more friends eager to hear her story. Invited into their elegant homes, she enlarged her circle of sympathetic donors. In 1858, Harriet spoke in Concord, Massachusetts, to luminaries of the literary and antislavery cultural scene. Louisa May Alcott, the future author of the bestselling novel *Little Women*, may have been present, as her parents were part of this social set. Alcott certainly saw Tubman in person the following year, 1859, when Tubman spoke before a large public audience. Harriet was visiting supporters and giving fundraising talks in Boston, the city where Alcott resided while working various domestic jobs and writing under a pseudonym.[7] Alcott, in her twenties at the time, was publishing adventure and mystery thrillers that she called her "blood and thunder tales." Hearing Tubman relate her story strengthened Alcott's abolitionist convictions, and inspired her, it seems, to produce short stories about interracial relationships.[8] Tubman's influence may have been part of the reason why Louisa May Alcott later left Massachusetts to work as a nurse in a Civil War hospital. Harriet would not have expected to impact the career of an up-and-coming woman writer, but she did intend for her story to spur the radical movement to which she was dedicating her life. Captivating an audience led to raising awareness as well as funds, both of which were critical to her rescues and to her vision of the future.

Harriet became an itinerant activist in these crucial antebellum years as the 1850s slid into the 1860s. Much like the Black holy women who traveled across state and national lines to preach and hold prayer meetings in this era, Harriet often took to the road. She continued to perform domestic labor in different locations in order to earn an income. She carried out rescue work in rural and urban Maryland, stopping through Delaware to resupply at Thomas Garrett's, and regrouping in Philadelphia. She traveled to Concord and Boston to raise funds and reinforce ties. And she helped the people she guided north to settle into their new communities. "Her efforts were not confined to the escape of slaves," Ednah Cheney wrote. "She conducted them to Canada, watched over their welfare, collected clothing, organized them into societies, and was always occupied with plans for their benefit."[9]

All along the way as she captained escapes and supplied freedom settlements, Harriet spread her version of God's intentions. A few years after she began working with William Still and Thomas Garrett in the Wilmington-Philadelphia network, she left that area to resettle outside Auburn, New York. A free state on the international border with Canada, New York would be a safer and more efficient location for her transnational rescue operation. Just as importantly, Auburn was a town upstate where Harriet had personal connections and could expect to tap into a politically committed social network. She had met Frances Seward, a white abolitionist and feminist from that town, through her contacts with the abolitionist Lucretia Coffin Mott of Philadelphia, and her sister Martha Coffin. Frances was married to William H. Seward, an antislavery advocate, a former New York governor, current U.S. senator, and secretary of state in Abraham Lincoln's administration starting in 1861. In addition to their part-time residence in Washington, DC (where Frances would spend little time), the Sewards resided in an ornate mansion on a four-acre lot in the city of Auburn. The couple owned additional properties that they rented and sold as economic investments. Leveraging her family wealth and marriage to advance her desire to actively aid the abolitionist movement, as the biographer Dorothy Wickenden argues, Frances likely urged William (called Henry by his friends) to give Harriet the chance to purchase a home. The Sewards had inherited a seven-acre farm from Frances's father, Elijah Miller, that was sitting vacant on the edge of town. This land had been in Frances Miller Seward's family since the late 1700s and passed into her husband's legal control upon the death of her father in 1851. In mid-spring of 1859 when the trees and tulips would have bloomed with color, William Seward's young adult son and namesake executed the transaction. Acting at the behest of his mother and on behalf of his father, who was away on an international trip, William Seward Jr. sold the farm, complete with a small wood frame house, to Harriet Tubman.[10]

Side view of Harriet Tubman's home in Auburn, New York. A handwritten inscription on the back reads: "Harriet Tubman Davis? Home / Side view of Here [sic] Home on South St. / Auburn N.Y." (The original wood plank house was replaced by a brick house following a fire.)

Collection of the Smithsonian National Museum of African American History and Culture, Gift of Charles L. Blockson.

Harriet Tubman's barn. A handwritten inscription on the back reads: "The barn on her Place. / Harriet Tubman / the last of the barns on her personal / estate."

Collection of the Smithsonian National Museum of African American History and Culture, Gift of Charles L. Blockson.

The Sewards' sale of the house and land with a mortgage attached attested to the family's trust in Harriet and their commitment to the antislavery cause. The lot they sold

Harriet was larger than some others they owned and situated in a rural spot just beyond the city limits.[11] But this was not a wholly unique land deal for the Sewards, and Tubman was not the only Black woman they did business with. Family letters indicate that Seward and his sons sold and rented multiple properties in the area to buyers and tenants of different racial backgrounds and kept careful notations about property values as related to sale prices and rents. The Sewards did not inflate the price of the land that they sold to Harriet Tubman, but neither did they give her a discount. William Seward Jr. wrote in an accounting to his father about the deal:

> On the 25th of May I sold the house to Harriet Tubman (a colored woman from Rochester) with seven acres of land for $1200. the house you will remember cost $500. and you valued the land at $100. per a[cre] She has already made a payt of $225. on her contract and promises another $100 by the first of Sept This I think is a larger payment than has ever been made down on any of the lots heretofore sold. Do you wish to sell any more of the land at the same price (100 per a[cre])? I think I can find a customer for another lot of the same size.[12]

Although the Sewards thought $1,200 ($40,000 today) was a fair and even generous price for a prime lot, they acted at least in part on a profit motive as they engaged in the sale of valuable land just as their progenitor, Elijah Miller, a land speculator, had done before them. They saw Tubman's lot as one among others that could produce income.[13] And for her part, Tubman seems to have been glad for the opportunity to enter the home ownership market. Possessing and managing her own home had been a dream that she was finally able to realize with the Sewards' sponsorship. Her investment made Tubman a trailblazer in a "determined diaspora of Black landowners [who] began to step out from the ruins of slavery," acquiring property through "backbreaking effort."[14] Black-owned plots dotting the American landscape from east to west would later support extended families, anchor communities, and seed settlements during and after the period of Reconstruction.

The town of Auburn and nearby settlements were located near a chain of long interior lakes where Cayuga people had lived for generations. This fertile land that the Sewards sold was morally encumbered, then, by a history of Indigenous dispossession. Judge Elijah Miller, William Seward's father-in-law, had himself inherited the property from his father, Josiah Miller, who fought in the American

Revolutionary War and received a government land grant for service. That war had gone well for American patriots but disastrously for Haudenosaunee people of the Iroquois Confederacy, also known as the Six Nations, made up of the Senecas, Cayugas, Onandagas, Oneidas, Mohawks, and Tuscaroras, who lived throughout the state of New York and Ontario (and in different periods in North Carolina—the Tuscaroras, and in Wisconsin—the Oneidas). As a confederacy, the Six Nations attempted to maintain neutrality during the war between the English colonies and Great Britain, though individual nations and bands aligned with the British. In 1779, George Washington ordered Continental Army forces to attack Cayuga and Seneca towns in order to weaken groups he saw as allies to the enemy. This incursion, led by Major General John Sullivan, brought four brigades of rampaging soldiers into Indigenous territory, resulting in the destruction of two dozen villages and the displacement of five thousand Seneca and Cayuga people. Following this attack and even before the war had ended, New York state, and then the new federal government, rushed to obtain Haudenosaunee land for Euro-American settlement and financial speculation, pushing the allied nations into a series of treaties. New York state partitioned a large tract of land originally belonging to Haudenosaunee people "to distribute as bounties to the state's soldiers."[15] It was Josiah Miller's reward of a plot in this Central New York Military Tract that initially drew the Miller family to the region.[16] Harriet Tubman's farm, which had formerly been the Seward-Miller family's land, rightfully belonged to displaced Cayuga people. The acres on which she would build her free haven were, in truth, ill-gotten gains.[17]

Harriet may not have known the precise derivation of her property when she purchased it nearly eighty years after the American Revolutionary War. But Haudenosaunee people still lived dispersed and in pockets across the state. Attuned as she was to her environments and the power relations embedded in places, Harriet must have realized some aspect of this past. Beyond the shadowed nature of the original conveyance of her property from Cayuga to New York owners, Harriet faced the additional weight of personal indebtedness. After scraping together a significant down payment, she plunged into homeownership reliant on credit. When she accepted the mortgage William Seward Jr. offered, she did not know where she would get the money to pay the principal and recurring interest each term. She could have failed to raise the next amount due and lost the farm along with her financial investment of the down payment. In this, too, she trusted in God and His plan to provide for her. Her leap into debt was another sign of her faith. It was also evidence of her burning desire to own land and a home of her own from which she could stage her rescues and live out her creed of freedom.

Settling in Auburn also placed Harriet fairly near St. Catharines, Ontario, where she had established a home for her parents, Rit and Ben. As a teenager, Harriet had repeatedly dreamt of the borderline. As a grown woman, she lived near and across geographical borders, regional and national in scope. She knew that crossing into a new environment, no matter how frightening, could mean the difference between bondage and freedom. Her ability to cover the miles by various means—from foot, to wagon, to rail, to boat—had been honed through experience. Her willingness to do so was a character trait formed out of both adversity and opportunity. She had always moved as a child who was frequently leased out by her owners. And she learned to subsist and then to resist in foreign environments, recognizing that these places sometimes yielded new tools for the struggle.

In the North, as in the South, Harriet continued to navigate by dream, allowing the pictures in her head to guide her. In the spring of 1858, she met with John Brown in St. Catharines, Ontario. John had decided to orchestrate a raid on Harpers Ferry, a federal arsenal in Virginia, as a means of spurring enslaved men to rise up, prompt a race war, and overthrow the demon Slavery. He had been making his own Northeastern circuit over the preceding months, visiting with abolitionists in New York and Boston to garner support and funds. In Ontario, he was hoping to recruit formerly enslaved Black men, who had freed themselves, to act as his advance guard of combatants. John, who was himself an intensely religious person, had heard about Harriet's background and saw her as a potential adviser. He seems to have felt an immediate respect upon meeting Harriet, whom he referred to as General Tubman and described as "one of the best and bravest persons on this continent."[18]

But this occasion in St. Catharines was not the first time Harriet had met John. Prior to that in-person encounter, she had a dream or vision in which she saw his likeness. In the dream, "she thought she was in 'a wilderness sort of place, all full of rocks, and bushes,' when she saw a serpent raise its head among the rocks, and as it did so, it became the head of an old man with a long white beard, gazing at her, 'wishful like, just as if he was going to speak to me.'" This dream, which had recurred over a period of time before the actual first meeting of the pair, ended with "a great crowd of men rush[ing] in and strik[ing] down the younger heads and then the head of the old man," who appeared to still be gazing at her with hope.[19] Harriet agreed to help John recruit among the men who had relocated from her home counties of

Dorchester and Caroline, Maryland, and she met with them in her residence that spring. Some of these men joined John Brown's movement. But in the summer of 1859, Harriet did not follow through with her promise to personally gather recruits for Brown. One of their mutual abolitionist friends, Franklin Sanborn, told John Brown that Harriet was "probably . . . sick."[20] This may have been accurate, given Harriet's battle with repeated and chronic illness, or it could have been an excuse, hinting at the possibility that Harriet felt, even if she did not express it, a sense of warning in her recurring dream of John Brown. The dream was replete with biblical symbolism. In it, Harriet saw the wilderness, or the place of trial and testing where one must find and lean on God. She also saw a serpent, representative of Satan in the Garden of Eden, the original deceiver. While Harriet was deeply fond of John because of his fervent defense of her people and, likely, his similarly fierce Christian belief, some part of her must have doubted his plan. In October of 1859, John Brown and his fighting force, including two of his sons and one Black man from Chatham, Ontario, near St. Catharines, raided the federal arsenal.[21] They were surrounded by U.S. marines. Many of the rebels were killed. John Brown himself would be tried and hanged for treason.

Harriet Tubman admired and revered John Brown. "Her

own veneration of Captain Brown has always been profound," Sarah Bradford wrote.[22] And yet, she did not follow his lead. Instead, she seems again to have followed what she felt were messages from God. Still, Harriet found a way to interpret John's death through her lens of faith. "I've been studying and studying upon it," she told Ednah Cheney, "and it's clear to me, it wasn't John Brown that died on that gallows. When I think of how he gave up his life for our people, and how he never flinched, but was so brave to the end; it's clear to me it wasn't mortal man, it was God in him." Harriet processed this ordeal as a thinker who had "studied" her mind and as a believer who had acted on faith under pressure. She saw John as a person very much like herself, a spiritual sibling acting on behalf of God and through whom God acted. Just as she had once said she was ready to die when God had no more use for her, she saw John Brown's death as having been permitted by God. He was a vessel carrying God's will, a second hand on the face of God's clock. And she was, too.

Harriet may have been preparing herself for the call to give up her earthly life as soon as she heard that John had been hanged for his armed attack on racial slavery. In 1859, nothing was at all clear about the future demise of slavery or even the advent of a war. But Harriet, again attuned to God's messaging, claimed to have known that a battle would come. Long before the war broke out with the firing of Confederate guns from the Charleston, South Carolina, harbor toward Fort Sumter, Harriet was in the middle of one of her travel circuits. She was in New York, staying in the home of the Reverend Henry Highland Garnet, when she had what she experienced as a visual precognition. "A vision came to her in the night of the emancipation of her people," Bradford wrote. "Whether a dream, or one of those glimpses into the future, which sometimes seem to have been granted to her, no one can say."[23]

The Civil War erupted within a few years of Harriet's vision. Feeling compelled to serve in the Union effort, which she saw as God's move to free the people through Lincoln's army, Harriet left the comforts of home to further the cause. At the personal urging of the governor of Massachusetts, John A. Andrew, who felt her skills would be useful, she traveled south once more. Harriet sacrificed yet again to answer this call of duty, which carried political as well as spiritual stakes in her view. Back in Auburn, she left behind not only her grown relatives but also Margaret Stewart, a beloved niece (or quite possibly, daughter) around ten years old whom she had recently brought from Maryland under mysterious circumstances. Before her departure, Harriet situated Margaret in the home of Frances Seward, who acted as Margaret's guardian.[24]

In the spring of 1862, Harriet traveled to the southeastern Sea Islands, where Union troops had taken control of large swaths of island territory, while inland, Confederate forces still held sway. As an individual on special assignment, she joined the personnel of the Department of the South, commanded by Major General David Hunter. The department encompassed South Carolina, Georgia, and Florida. It was headquartered on Hilton Head Island and also conducted operations on Port Royal Island in the town of Beaufort. In Beaufort, where she was primarily stationed, Harriet entered a different set of social and ecological relationships, applying skills she had already honed to a new terrain that sounded environmental echoes of her Eastern Shore homeland.

Everywhere she turned, Harriet's can-do skills were called upon. Refugees from slavery who had made their way to the Union camps were desperate for food, shelter, medical care, and opportunities to support themselves as they navigated the dangers of war and uncertainties about their status. Military commanders and officers were eager for intelligence about the capacities and movements of Confederate troops on the mainland. Soldiers were desperate for treatment after contracting diseases and suffering battlefield wounds. Harriet

Tubman stepped into the space of all these needs, practicing an ethic of care developed in New York and drawing on offensive and defensive talents shaped on the secretive Underground Railroad. She had been sent south by Governor Andrew and was under the command of General Benjamin F. Butler. At the same time, she operated with a great degree of autonomy, applying her own solutions to problems she encountered and traveling with official passes for free military transport by 1865.[25] Her first post was at the Christian Commission, where she distributed supplies sent by the New England Freedmen's Aid Society. For a brief time after she first arrived, Harriet drew modest pay from the military, which she used to establish a washhouse and eatery. She taught Black women who had emancipated themselves how to launder for wages in the facility, while offering advice on finding work in a free market economy. [26]

At field hospitals in South Carolina and nearby Florida, she bathed Black soldiers' wounds and treated their illnesses as a military nurse. In this essential endeavor, she drew upon her ecological knowledge of medicinal plants that grew along coastlines.[27] Bradford wrote of Tubman's work as a healer: "She nursed our soldiers in the hospitals, and knew how, when they were dying by numbers of some malignant disease, with cunning skill to extract from roots and herbs, which grew near the source of the disease, the healing draught,

which allayed the fever and restored numbers to health."
Harriet sourced this natural cure for dysentery "from roots
which grew near the waters which gave the disease," Bradford said. Ednah Cheney offered additional detail about Tubman's insistence on making and distributing these remedies
for free: "She has also been making herb-medicine for the
soldiers, which she gives away gratuitously."[28] While Tubman cared for soldiers with organic medicines she had
concocted, she also cooked for cash. Much like the years
when she had worked to fund her rescue missions, she continued doing domestic labor—in this case baking "cakes and
pies for sale, in the intervals of her work" and making "casks
of root beer"—to support herself while she buttressed the
U.S. military.[29]

Harriet Tubman's best known, and perhaps most essential, wartime action was the role she played as a military
scout and spy. By mapping the area in her mind, recruiting
trustworthy allies, and fading into the social landscape as
she was accustomed to doing as a veteran Underground
Railroad operative, she contributed valuable intelligence.
Harriet organized a group of nine Black men, most of whom
had self-emancipated and hailed from the area, into a mobile
unit under her command. These men knew the terrain and
could describe the lay of the land in detail, pinpointing Confederate positions, while Harriet could travel undetected

among Black populations on reconnaissance missions. "Her closely knit band became an official scouting service for the Department of the South," the historian Catherine Clinton has written.[30] And Harriet's "spy ring" likely contributed intelligence that informed a daring water operation in South Carolina's intercoastal zone, now known as the Combahee River Raid.[31]

Colonel James Montgomery, who had recently taken command of the Second Regiment, South Carolina Volunteers, a newly formed unit of the Department of the South, earned formal credit for the raid. Like Tubman, Montgomery was a staunch Christian and abolitionist who deeply admired the deceased John Brown. And both Harriet and James had known John personally. James Montgomery had allied with John Brown in Kansas, protecting antislavery settlers in that state and conducting raids against proslavery settlers across the Missouri border in the 1850s. He brought experience with these guerilla war tactics to South Carolina.[32] Montgomery's plan, to which other colleagues in his inner circle contributed, was to conduct a surprise raid on a series of rice plantations on the marshy wetlands between the Sea Islands and the mainland. In this water-swept region, one of the most lucrative in the state, thousands of people were enslaved to produce a crop that yielded both food for residents and riches for enslavers. Montgomery had intertwined objectives in launching this audacious mission. He wanted to weaken Confederate forces in South Carolina; he wanted to punish enslavers; and he wanted to free enslaved people who could then reinforce the Union ranks.[33] And Tubman may have influenced his strategy of stealth maneuvering. "A sneak attack in the dead of night, to catch slaveholders off guard in their own backyards, was vintage Tubman," Clinton has written.[34]

On June 1 of 1863, Montgomery's force of approximately three hundred men and at least one woman set off for a nighttime assault on a heavily defended area via the Combahee, a narrow, winding tidal river. Beneath a moonless sky, they traveled on three military-grade steamboats: the *Sentinel*, the *John Adams*, and the *Harriet A. Weed*. The goal was to follow the river near the coastline, pausing to land small advance teams. These men would identify and neutralize enemy soldiers at fortifications along the way while the large ships progressed up the river, fired on plantations, and released soldiers onto the seagrass bordering the rice fields. Immediately, though, the plan went awry as their contingent of three vessels was reduced to two. The *Sentinel* had run off course and become grounded. The fighters consolidated on the remaining ships with the *John Adams* at the lead. Beside Colonel James Montgomery in the pilothouse stood Harriet Tubman in her long dark dress beneath an even darker sky.[35]

This was a terrain that Tubman and her scout ring knew well. At least two of her men, Charles Simmons and Samuel Hayward (who had absconded from one of these rice plantations), were with her onboard. As the ships advanced, firing on the plantation grounds from the water channel, soldiers sloshed through the wetlands to storm the estates on shore, burning plantation houses and rice fields while preserving the cabins of the enslaved. During the Combahee River operation, hundreds of enslaved people heard the boom of the Union guns and rushed toward the soggy bank, carrying their children and their belongings, including animals, foodstuffs, and cooking pots, even as overseers chased them with threats and whips. The people seeking to free themselves were struck by confusion and panic, nearly overwhelming the crew as they attempted to leap toward the decks of the boats.[36] To project calm and encourage order, Colonel Montgomery asked Harriet Tubman, whom he called Moses, to sing. Harriet threw her distinctive voice into the chaotic air, choosing a popular antislavery hymn. The notes rose over the din of gunfire, screams, and shouts. She sang to these desperate, determined people as she had sung to many like them before, conveying a message of confidence and hope: "Come along! Come along! don't be alarmed, Uncle Sam is rich enough to give you all a farm." The crowd was reassured upon hearing the promise of safety and land sung by this stranger, a Black holy woman from parts unknown. With greater clarity and calm, they boarded the rowboats let down by the ships. Something about the singer inspired trust, perhaps a tremor in her voice, or a glint of divine love in her eyes. This performance became, again, a ritual of call and response that Harriet had enacted before on routes of escape. After she uttered each line of her impromptu song, Harriet heard the people shout "Glory." Sensing that the people felt the presence of God in this moment would have been more important to Harriet than knowing, as we do now, that she

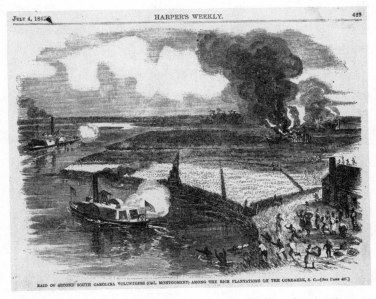

Drawing of the Combahee River Raid, *Harper's Weekly*, July 4, 1863.

was the first known woman to play a leadership role in an armed raid in the U.S. military.[37] To her mind, that historic achievement would have paled behind her mission to lead God's freedom charge.

More than seven hundred souls were liberated that day by the Combahee River raiders. Confederate soldiers, slaveholders, and overseers confronted scenes of destruction in the background alight with fire and smoke. As the gunboats skimmed back down the channel, weighted down by passengers and things, the sky opened over them. A storm burst from the realms above, flashing thunder, roiling the river, and churning the ocean beyond. But Harriet Tubman had seen this before—a stormy night and righteous quest accompanied by a saving grace—and she was in her element.[38]

When news of the raid traveled up Colonel Montgomery's chain of command and out to the Northern press, astonishment merged with celebration. Montgomery was heralded as a "gallant" hero for having caught the Confederates unaware, disrupting their operations, reducing their resources, and freeing hundreds of people. And Harriet Tubman was described in one newspaper, without being named, as "a Black she 'Moses.'" Abolitionist Franklin Sanborn responded to this anonymizing coverage by printing Tubman's name, a sketch of her life, and part of a letter she had sent in his publication, the *Commonwealth*.[39]

Tubman's dictated letter to Sanborn revealed her pride in the mission but also her feeling that she and her scouts had not received their due. "Don't you think we colored people are entitled to some credit for that exploit, under the lead of the brave Colonel Montgomery?" she asked. "We weakened the rebels somewhat on the Combahee River, by taking and bringing away seven hundred and fifty-six head of their most valuable live stock, known up in your region as 'contrabands,' and this, too, without the loss of a single life on our part, though we had a good reason to believe that a number of rebels bit the dust."[40] In this missive, Harriet showed a side of herself that is often submerged in the as-told-to biographies—the laser-sharp critic with a keen understanding of racial politics and perhaps a thirst for vengeance. She also described her mission outfit, in keeping with many other examples in which clothing captured her attention—from her purchase of a new suit of clothes for John Tubman to her love of a silk dress to a personal style described by Ednah Cheney as liking "to dress handsomely."[41] Here Harriet called out her own apparel as being inadequate for the task at hand.

In our late expedition up the Combahee River, in coming on board the boat, I was carrying two pigs for a poor sick woman, who had a child to carry, and the order 'double quick' was given, and I started to run, stepped on my dress, it being rather long, and fell and tore it almost off, so that when I got on board the boat there was hardly any thing left of it but shreds. I made up my mind then I would never wear a long dress on another expedition of the kind, but would have a bloomer as soon as I could get it.[42]

It was typical of Harriet to be so focused on the needs of others in the moment, lugging the two swine to help an over-burdened mother, that she tripped in the process. She also announced that she desired the practical, split-leg garment that was becoming a visible signifier of women's independence. Here, too, her commentary was social critique, highlighting the confining clothing women were expected to wear. Harriet had said, before the war: "The good Lord has come down to deliver my people, and I must go and help him."[43] Carrying out God's mission, in her view, left room for social analysis, for vanquishing enemies with the sword, and for women's unabashed leadership.

Harriet Tubman had assured the fleeing Combahee River residents (whose individual biographies and complex histories are carefully reconstructed in a new book by the historian and descendant Edda Fields-Black) that they would have farms provided by the government.[44] She did not know that "Uncle Sam" would ultimately break faith with formerly enslaved people and their children, denying them the proverbial forty acres and a mule as the war progressed. In the fall of 1865, President Andrew Johnson revoked land that had been confiscated from enslavers and redistributed to Black residents of the Sea Islands by General William T. Sherman in Field Order No. 15, crushing their hopes and rendering them homeless. The removal of federal troops from the South after 1877 left freed people even more vulnerable to physical, economic, and political abuses. If God was faithful and trustworthy in Tubman's experience, the United States government would later prove that it was not. Did Harriet have an inkling of the dark years ahead, as described by W. E. B. Du Bois in his classic history, *Black Reconstruction*: "Then came this battle called the Civil War . . . The slave went free; stood a brief moment in the sun; then moved back again toward slavery. The whole weight of America was thrown to color caste."[45] Did she receive a vision about this dim future of political exclusion and racial violence in the post-Reconstruction era rife with lynchings and riotous attacks on Black communities? And was it too much to bear, too terrible to speak of, after what she had already been through? Perhaps Harriet Tubman, a front-lines healer and commander now, had seen enough of gore and gloom on the battlefield. Perhaps her thoughts turned to her farm in

New York, where relatives and friends awaited her return. Harriet's dictated letter to Franklin Sanborn indicated that she longed for home. "I have now been absent two years almost, and have just got letters from my friends in Auburn, urging me to come home. My father and mother are old and in feeble health, and need my care and attention."[46]

7

THE CARETAKER

My ardour for the progress of his cause abates
not a whit,

so far as I am able to judge,

though I am now something more than fifty years of age.

—JARENA LEE, *THE LIFE AND RELIGIOUS EXPERIENCE
OF JARENA LEE, A COLOURED LADY*, 1836

We must always seek first God's vision and live our lives
into that good tomorrow. This is our song of hope that
leads us home, leads us home.

—EMILIE M. TOWNES, "ETHICS AS AN ART OF
DOING THE WORK OUR SOULS MUST HAVE,"
WOMANIST THEOLOGICAL ETHICS, 2011

Harriet returned to New York having done what she set out to do on that fall day in 1849 when she crossed the Pennsylvania border. She had played an outsize role in setting her people free. And in her winter years, the long, next phase of her life between the 1860s and 1890s, she planned, built, and tended an intentional community of the redeemed. Harriet had come a long way from the girl called Minty who slept and ate with the piglets, but she still felt a continued closeness with the natural and nonhuman world around her. The location of her snug farmette, perched on the outer edge of Auburn, had features in common with the Eastern Shore of her youth. In this region, as in Maryland, waterways carried the memories of Indigenous peoples and concepts: the Choptank River, Nanticoke River, and Susquehanna River were echoed by Canandaigua Lake, Seneca Lake, Cayuga Lake, Owasco Lake, Skaneateles Lake, and Otisco Lake. While far from the Atlantic coast, this new place had water in abundance. Auburn was one among many nineteenth-century towns established in the lush Finger Lakes zone within the traditional homelands of the Cayuga people and the Haudenosaunee Confederacy. There were fresh bodies of blue water teeming with fish. There were green fields and thick forests. There were ample friends and relatives. There was a kind of peace. Harriet had moved her parents from St. Catharines to her home in Auburn before leaving to serve in the war. As she said to Ednah Cheney: "I sold my silk gown to go after my mother."[1] Harriet remarried in 1869, to a younger Union Army veteran named Nelson Davis. Perhaps she was as attached to him as she had once been to John Tubman, her first husband of over twenty years earlier. If so, she did not describe those intimate feelings to biographers, as seems to have been her preference. She also adopted a daughter, Gertie Davis, and enjoyed spending time with extended kin. "Her little house was always neat and comfortable, and the small parlor was nicely and rather prettily furnished," Bradford wrote. Harriet's home must have been a cozy place, scented with the gingerbread and fruit pies that she was expert at baking.[2] We can imagine that milk and honey (or sweet milk and sugar lumps) abounded there for the taking when funds afforded.

But there was also tension and hardship in the community Harriet built. Money was difficult to earn for African Americans attempting to compete in the workforce populated by thousands of new European immigrants in an economy tainted by color prejudice. Obtaining supplies for daily life was a challenge, too. Harriet opened her sturdy brick home to people in need, unsure of where food would come from but continuing to trust in her God. To Harriet's mind, it was God who led neighbors to bring by baskets of vittles or associates from her conducting days to drop cash into the mail with letters. She might have thought the same about the Tlingit girls at the Fort Wrangell boarding school for Indigenous youth in Alaska, who raised and sent $37 after reading about her story in a missionary periodical even amid what must have been a trying experience of assimilative schooling.[3] Given that Harriet lived on land that was originally territory of the still proximal Haudenosaunee people, it is hard to believe that members of those communities did not at times also offer help. "She takes in destitute and infirm colored people and takes care of them. How she does that is as a mystery . . . but she claims that the Lord sends the means as she needs them," wrote Elizabeth Chace, an associate of

Tubman's in Auburn. "'The Lord will provide' was her motto, and He never failed her," wrote Sarah Bradford about Tubman's efforts in New York.[4]

Emma Telford told a story that she presented as characteristic, which captured not only Tubman's persistent faith in God but also her redefinition of what it meant to be blessed. Telford wrote: "Reaching the house one morning I found Harriet in great cheer. 'How do you think the Lord has answered my prayer this here morning,' she asked? 'The meal chest was empty last night, so I prayed all night "Lord send me thy blessing. Thou knowest what they servant needs. Send me a blessing."' Harriet stepped into the yard and 'met that blessing a comin in, and what do you think it was? A poor blind woman bad off with consumption, and her six little children one of them just a baby." Harriet then "did just what the Lord meant for [her] to do." She canvassed her neighbors on South Street to collect food and clothing for the family, whom she had taken in.[5] Harriet's brothers must have contributed to this collective pantry.

With the help of others, Harriet was a benefactor for many. She managed a combination boardinghouse and assisted living center in her modest home. She saw her guests as blessings rather than burdens and did not charge for their stays. Profit had never been her motive—as a military nurse and pharmacist, public storyteller, or private homeowner.

When she acquired things that she loved or viewed as valuable, she was willing to share or part with them, as she had done with the "old silk dress . . . given her among a bundle of clothes."[6] And while Harriet seems to have monitored her income and expenses, she sometimes made errors in judgment. Bradford commented that Harriet could be overgenerous when it came to spending on visitors in need, such that a woman in the neighborhood took it upon herself to ration out cash sent to her by donors for Harriet. In 1873, when Harriet was in her fifties, she was deceived by a pair of con men promising gold. Against the advice of her friends, she agreed to meet with these men in an isolated area where they stole the money they had convinced her to invest with them and beat her.[7] This awful incident does raise questions about Harriet's lowered guard in this stage of life and about how she would have interpreted the attack, given her belief in God's guidance.

But Harriet regrouped after this setback, for she had built a resilient community and expanded her land base with the purchase of twenty-five adjacent acres in 1896. In the final decades of her distinctive life, the great leader of an underground freedom network invested in an aboveground social network rooted in Black-owned land that functioned as communal space. Other holy women like her had thrived in community once their travels slowed, establishing informal circles of support and formal institutions while feeling that they did their Lord's work. Julia Foote settled in Cleveland, Ohio, and "praise[d] God through all eternity" for sending her there. Elizabeth moved to Michigan, where she "found a wide field of labour amongst [her] own color." Over the course of four years, Elizabeth opened an orphanage for Black youth, "having always felt the great importance of religious and moral agriculture of children."[8] Elizabeth's creative choice of wording there again underscores the role

Harriet Tubman at around the age of sixty-five, wearing a long skirt, shawl, and bandanna. Photo by Seymour Squyer, Auburn, New York, circa 1885.

National Portrait Gallery, Smithsonian Institution, open access.

of nature in these women's sense of godly purpose. To the northeast in New York, Harriet Tubman raised funds to pay for the farm and house through the sale of her as-told-to biography written by Sarah Bradford and first published in 1869. Bradford would later publish a second edition with the proceeds going to Harriet. Following the death of William Henry Seward, the Seward family forgave the balance due on Tubman's home loan. And after years of applying and being turned down, she finally acquired a steady income—a government pension of $20 per month for "her valuable services as nurse and scout during the wa[r] of the Rebellion."[9]

Harriet, her home, her dreams, and her land were social magnets. People came to seek her out, and all could find shelter under her roof. "In her own home Harriet delights to welcome any who may come," Emma Telford wrote, "opening her treasury of story and song."[10] Harriet maintained and expanded her welcoming home base in New York through the end of the nineteenth century and into the twentieth. In the late 1880s and 1890s, when she was in her sixties and seventies, her political scope widened to incorporate women's suffrage, and her network stretched to include the feminist campaigners Susan B. Anthony and Elizabeth Cady Stanton. She frequently attended feminist meetings in New York and Boston.[11] Harriet's dream in late life was to acquire enough land to establish a home and health-care center for people who were ill, elderly, or living with disabilities. She would ultimately accomplish this goal, placing twenty-five acres and several buildings under the care of the African Methodist Episcopal Zion Church where she worshipped. Harriet named the main building in the complex John Brown Hall. The second building would be called the Harriet Tubman Home for the Aged, after its founder. In 1913, Harriet died in John Brown Hall, within the haven she had created, having been useful to God, as she would have seen it, for nearly a century.[12]

Harriet Tubman's personal household continued to reflect her lifelong mission of emancipation and care. These two aims and states of being were linked in Harriet's view of the good life. Her vision was not hers alone, though her example of it may be the boldest. Tubman's life choices and means of carrying them out reflected a shared outlook of Black Christian women who had endured captivity, fought for physical and spiritual freedom, and embraced "survival and a positive quality of life for black women and their families in the presence and care of God," as the theologian Delores Williams has put it.[13] Tubman's worldview was one of "responsible freedom," that recognized living in liberty required tending spirits, soothing hearts, and putting food on the table.[14] She believed in the practice of liberty's upkeep, which we might also call survival. Zilpha Elaw may have been thinking along similar lines when she told readers of her memoir: "May all who are of the household of faith stand fast in the liberty wherewith Christ has made them free." If faith was a household with freedom for floorboards, it required maintenance. And in this work of tending and caretaking, Elizabeth said in her memoir, God was her "almighty Helper."[15]

The women abolitionists who told Tubman's story were witness to this ethic of liberation care, but they did not all recognize the underlying philosophy or intentionality of those scenes. Instead, they saw Harriet and her friends as strange and quaint. On one occasion when Sarah Bradford visited, she was astonished (and somewhat appalled) by the array of people staying inside the brick home: "The lame, the halt and the blind, the bruised and crippled little children, and one crazy woman." Emma Telford wrote in a similar vein: "All these years her doors have been open to the needy, the most utterly friendless, and helpless of her race. The aged, forsaken by their own kith and kin, [sic] The babe deserted, the demented, the epileptic, the blind, the paralyzed, the consumptive all have found shelter and welcome. At no time can I recall the little home to have sheltered less than six or eight wrecks of humanity entirely dependent upon Harriet for their all."[16]

Harriet Tubman understood something that Sarah Bradford and Emma Telford missed, and that we must not overlook as we near the end of this faith biography. Every person had innate value and deserved care in the eyes of Harriet, who attempted to view the world through the lens of her God, an "almighty Helper." And beyond this, limitations and disabilities visible to the unenlightened might not be exactly what they seemed. After all, Harriet herself, who had suffered from seizures since early adolescence, had always somehow maintained a keen awareness of her social and natural contexts. Perhaps her seeming bouts of unconsciousness had simultaneously been periods of inner wakefulness that kept her attuned to the shimmering potential of all life.

In a story told to showcase Harriet Tubman's humor, Harriet's relative remembered hearing that Tubman, who often fell asleep in a chair in the corner, was conscious most of that time, taking in the sounds and sensations of her environment. "[S]he pretended to be asleep . . . but she knew everything that was going on in the room because she'd wake up and continue the conversation. Or make some comment about something they'd said . . . they thought she was asleep, and she really wasn't," Judith Bryant shared. "Supposedly Harriet said every shut eye ain't sleep, every good bye ain't gone."[17] Things are not always as they appear. Harriet Tubman, for whom unseen powers reigned until she took her last breath, believed this.

This mysterious hidden nature of things could surface in surprising ways. When Harriet was a young enslaved woman working the land of the Eastern Shore, she hired an attorney to investigate the legal status of her mother, suspecting their owner of deceit. The lawyer found that Harriet's mother, Rit Green, should have been freed at the age of forty-five in accordance with the will of her first owner (Atthow Pattison, the great-grandfather of Edward Brodess). After that 1791 will went through probate in 1797, Rit's legal status changed from the category of a lifelong slave (the norm across the South and in Maryland) to the category of a "term slave" with a limited number of years claimed by her owner.[18] Term slavery was a complex status that included a variety of legal permutations, including that an enslaved Black woman's children born before the start and end of her term would most likely be relegated to lifelong captivity.[19] However, the lawyer found that Rit's children were included in the provision, such that they would be freed at age forty-five, too. Harriet's youngest siblings born after their mother reached the stipulated age should have been free all along. This included Moses, the son Rit hid in the woods. "Harriet supposes the whole family were actually free, and were kept wrongfully in a state of slavery all those long years," Bradford wrote, "but she simply states the fact, without any mourning or lamenting over the wrong and the misery of it all, accepting it as the will of God, and, therefore, not to be rebelled against."[20] The story, as Tubman may have interpreted it, bears a hint of the biblical. Perhaps deep down in her bones, independent Minty Ross knew freedom had always belonged to her and her people. Perhaps this kernel of self-knowledge reinforced religious faith, shaping her sense of justice. Perhaps in slavery's pit of affliction, like a diamond forged under pressure of fire, Harriet the Caretaker was made.

Conclusion

THE ROCK

Aunt Harriet was supposed to be the rock in our family . . .
She's still our rock.

—GERALDINE COPES, GREAT-GRANDNIECE
OF HARRIET TUBMAN, 2011

Every goodbye ain't gone.

—A HARRIET TUBMAN SAYING PASSED
DOWN IN FAMILY MEMORY

Of all the abolitionist praise collected and printed as testimonials in the first full-length account of Harriet Tubman's life, Frederick Douglass's words are the most perceptive. Douglass named "the midnight sky and the silent stars" as witnesses to Tubman's actions, recognizing, as Tubman had insisted all along, that she did not make her stand alone. The stars had watched over her, and she would, in turn, observe their light, seeing in these gaseous bodies a host of incandescent messengers. "Harriet knew the North Star," her associate Helen Tatlock remembered; "that was one thing she insisted that she was *always* sure of."[1] Waterways had shored her up, too, welcoming Tubman into their depths and allowing her and her parties safe passage. Her most intimate natural allies seem to have been those sprung from the soil—weeds that defied ordered, hierarchical society, and trees that populated the forests where she walked, worked, and wended north. She may even have relied on landmark rocks to help her chart her course of escape, or rested on a flat, smooth stone like Baby Suggs in the novel *Beloved*. By the end of her life, she had herself become like these various features of nature: a guiding star, a giving tree, a saving river, and a bracing rock in the lives of the people who depended on her and on whom she could depend for companionship.

Harriet Tubman's relationship with entities of the natural world, of which she was also feelingly a part, was synergistic, empowering, and impactful. Her awareness of geographical positioning and her knowledge of how nature might come to her aid were second only to her faith in God and seemed at times to be fused with it. Following what she described as God's guidance, Harriet directed her companions to hide behind trees, within swamps, and in "potato holes."[2] She coaxed them to walk into rising creeks seemingly against reason. She taught them to listen for barred owl calls, which she would mimic as an "all-clear" sign.[3] Nature to Harriet was present and responsive. Just as she was a real woman and not a paper doll cutout, the trees, waters, stars, plants, and animals around her were spiritually material. When Harriet described to Bradford one particularly memorable approach to the Canadian border in the company of a fugitive group, she may have mentioned the landscape. Across that bridge, Bradford related, lay "Sweet fields beyond the swelling flood, All dressed in living green."[4] While Bradford drew these words from a hymn, the sentiment of land being vibrantly alive rings true to Tubman's character. Harriet made a friend of nature, just as she made a partner of God. She approached each day of living on earth with a luminous pragmatism.

Harriet Tubman's relationships with people (also natural life-forms as much as we often forget this) were as rich and diverse as her relationships with trees and other non-human beings. She grew up with a fierce love of family even as its members were picked apart. Her determination to free her relatives birthed a mission that mushroomed. She launched a campaign of liberating hundreds of others and caring for their needs. Slowly and painstakingly, she gathered more of those people around her, marrying, adopting, forming a community in upstate New York that echoed, but could never fully replicate, her ravaged childhood community back in Maryland. She made this reunion vision possible by anchoring that community on a tender piece of land with its own markings, erasures, and histories. Even with the heartrending losses she mourned on this ground (land that must have, in turn, mourned the loss of its original

Indigenous people), Harriet made gains. Kin-making and shelter-building became her chief aims after midlife. A descendant of the family, Harriet Tubman's great-grand-niece Judith Bryant, pointed out the importance of community and the misperception that Harriet was living out her last years alone. "Many people were under the impression she lived in Auburn all by her lonesome, poor thing . . . It was not the case. She was surrounded by family. And they took care of each other."[5] The family that Harriet Tubman had knit together was so extensive that it included not only birth relatives and adopted kin but nearly the whole town. "Everybody in Auburn called her Aunt Harriet," said another family descendant, Geraldine Copes. The practice was so widespread, and the ties so thick, that Copes, the youngest in the family, was surprised to learn in her twenties that Tubman was her great-aunt by blood.[6]

Harriet Tubman is one of the most widely recognized and celebrated women in United States history. Statues and plaques have been erected in her honor, and she is, according to a national survey cited by the historian Lois Horton, "among the top ten most famous people in American history."[7] In 2017, the state of Maryland established a crowning public commemoration of Tubman's achievements in the form of the Harriet Tubman Underground Railroad State Park and Visitor Center, a park and learning center aptly in-

tegrated into the natural surroundings, abutting the Blackwater National Wildlife Refuge. By 2021, the center had
hosted over 350,000 visitors from all the U.S. states and
over sixty other countries.[8] This multifaceted exhibit that
integrates landscape renders the complexity of Tubman's
life story and the freedom movement she championed.

Sunlight shining through a fork in the Tubman family's
memorial tree, two pines that have grown together over time.
Fort Hill Cemetery, Auburn, New York.

Photo by Tiya Miles, 2023.

Tubman's most graceful memorial, though, grows directly from the ground. In the early 1900s, in Auburn, New York, members of her family planted a testament to the memory of their deceased relatives. Said Judith Bryant: "The children . . . planted a small tree in Fort Hill. They thought it was a small Christmas tree and would stay forever small. And it is now the tallest tree in the cemetery. It's a Norway Spruce, and it is the landmark for the grave of Harriet Tubman."[9] Harriet's family memorial is evergreen, the plant that refused to stay small. And thus, a companion tree is once again this great woman's mirror.

Soon after she had seized her freedom and moved north, Harriet expressed sorrow at what she had left behind—the people, as well as the land: "I have no opportunity to see my friends in my native land," she said. "We would rather stay in our native land, if we could be as free there as we are here."[10] A deeply compassionate person propelled by her need for relational intimacy as well as her sense of moral duty, Harriet Tubman fought for the ability of all God's creatures to share this earth in freedom and dignity. Whether or not we hold her religious convictions, we bear witness to the power she unleashed by believing in something larger than herself. Harriet's love of family, friendship with trees, faith in God, and care for the needy were values united by a tenet of togetherness. She taught those who followed her into the woods to stay close and keep faith despite their fear of what lay behind *and* what lay ahead on the path. "The Lord had been with them in six troubles, and he would not desert them in the seventh," Harriet would say. God was with them. She was with them. The stars were with them, too. And wielding the powers of will and spirit, they would persist.

Beacon of Hope by Wesley Wofford depicts Harriet Tubman giving her younger self the key to remove a shackle while holding up the North Star. In 2022, the sculpture was placed in front of the Dorchester County Courthouse, once the site of slave auctions.

Photograph courtesy of Wesley Wofford © Wofford Sculpture Studio.

Incantation

———

RECALLING THE SPIRIT

the lord has been with me
in six troubles
he will not desert me
in the seventh

he will not desert me
in the seventh
the lord has been with me
in six

he will not
in the seventh
in six troubles
the lord

will not desert
me lord
in the seventh

the lord
will not desert

—QURAYSH ALI LANSANA, "INCANTATION,"
THEY SHALL RUN: HARRIET TUBMAN POEMS

The Ticket

—

A NOTE ON PROCESS AND SOURCES

I lay my hand on the shoulder of the writer of this letter, and I wish for you, and all your offsprings, a through ticket in the Gospel train to Glory.

—HARRIET TUBMAN REGARDING A DICTATED LETTER, SARAH BRADFORD, *SOME ADDITIONAL INCIDENTS IN THE LIFE OF HARRIET,* 1901

We may never fully recapture the past, but we can take on the struggles of those who came before, in the name of those who will come after, and in this way truly remember Harriet Tubman.

—CATHERINE CLINTON, *HARRIET TUBMAN: THE ROAD TO FREEDOM,* 2004

There have been and will be many tellers of Tubman's life story. Like me, they might wish they could feel the gentle press of her hand to their shoulder—the touch that Harriet may have believed would transfer her own intentions to the pen and page of the writer enlisted to capture her words. But without that guiding touch that may have helped to convey her ideas, we do our level best to dredge the historical record, a murky paper trail seeped through with porous channels like the coastal ground of the Eastern Shore where Tubman was born. To write this book, I have relied on swamped sources—materials about Tubman's life, often attributed to Tubman's oral accounts, which were also submerged in the perspectives and biases of others. This is the general state of the Tubman archive as well as the archive of enslaved people as a whole. The earliest texts we have for accessing details of Tubman's life, biographical treatments crafted in the nineteenth century, were produced by white women who knew Tubman, talked with Tubman, and took down notes, rather than by Tubman herself. These women saw themselves as Tubman's supporters. They shared political convictions with broader antislavery and feminist circles, lauded Tubman's courage, and intended to aid her by publishing her story. They aspired to an ideal of accuracy and noted their processes and sources. Sarah Bradford, Tubman's first official as-told-to biographer, said this about her methods in her 1869 account: "Many of the stories told me by Harriet, in answer to questions, have been corroborated by letters, some of which will appear in this book . . . I find among her papers, many of which are defaced by being carried with her for years, portions of letters addressed to myself, by persons at the South, and speaking of the valuable assistance Harriet was rendering our soldiers in the hospital."[1] Bradford and her fellow writers spoke to Tubman, double-checked sources, and reviewed documents. Nevertheless, these well-meaning women could not have told Tubman's story with the fullness, clarity, and philosophical depth that Tubman would have, had she written it herself. Because these early biographers could not possibly have rendered the whole truth, I have made room in my treatment for questions and skepticism, attempting to point out when these authors indicated they were summarizing, paraphrasing, or quoting Tubman's speech and to flush out their personal commentary and interpretations. These nineteenth-century biographers rendered Tubman's speech in their notion of Black regional dialect. However, we cannot know how Tubman sounded, and we cannot trust that biographers were capable of capturing her vocal style by way of the written word. What is more, even these women who spent hours interviewing and speaking with Tubman and felt themselves to be devoted to progressive causes could exhibit racial prejudice. In an abundance of caution, I have altered these quoted passages, shaking them free of excessive dialect. In making this choice, I realize that I am entering yet another discrepancy into the muddy Tubman record, but it is a compromise that I feel this account requires. (You may have noticed that I have only lightly edited dialect in the original words of the contemporary poet Quraysh Ali Lansana, who has adopted Harriet's fictionalized voice in a book of poems titled *They Shall Run*. In this case, I feel that creative license for a twenty-first-century Black poet who grasps the risks of dialect writing is warranted.)

A defining method in *Night Flyer*, one that is new so far as I know in treatments of Tubman's life, is my effort to consistently describe Tubman as part of a group of Black women who shared her deep religious conviction and took radical action to preach and act on what they believed was God's word. Threading my discussion of Tubman's life phases with the stories of Old Elizabeth, Jarena Lee, Zilpha Elaw, and Julia Foote, women the literary scholar William Andrews called "sisters of the spirit," was an effort not only to locate Tubman within a cohort of contemporaries but also to balance out the voices that would speak in the book and be heard by us.

This book stands on the evidentiary grounding of previous Tubman studies, and it relies more on a close reading of narrative texts than on an assembling of original documents (which, nevertheless, do appear sprinkled throughout). The archival foundation was built by other scholars whose work has been field defining for studies of Tubman and her network. Kate Clifford Larson's biography *Bound for the Promised Land: Harriet Tubman, Portrait of an American Hero* was an essential secondary source for this study. While visiting the Tubman site in Auburn, New York, I heard the senior tour guide cite Larson's work as definitive; this is a prevailing view among scholars and Tubman site practitioners with whom I have spoken. While new primary and artifactual materials may yet be found (especially in relation to Ben Ross's homesite and Anthony Thompson's acreage), and fresh interpretations always further our understanding of the past, it seems likely that much of Larson's meticulous portrait will remain intact. Kate Larson was also stunningly generous with her behind-the-scenes and off-the-page knowledge and resources, sharing numerous sources, ideas, late-breaking facts, and contacts with me. In this way, she has supported this telling as a quiet check and guide. Catherine Clinton's page-turner biography, *Harriet Tubman: The Road to Freedom*, is likewise essential to Tubman studies and was a model for my effort to vividly narrate Tubman's life. Both of these books are approaching their twentieth anniversary in 2023 (Larson) and 2024 (Clinton), which makes a new biographical effort like *Night Flyer* feel timely. I used Larson's and Clinton's works in tandem as major reference points, comparing them to address areas of confusion and gaps in the historical record, and sometimes bringing in more academic or specialized biographical and analytical studies, especially Jean M. Humez's literary historical monograph, *Harriet Tubman: The Life and the Life Stories* (also approaching a twentieth anniversary in 2023) and Lois E. Horton's *Harriet Tubman and the Fight for Freedom: A Brief History with Documents*. Shorter, recent treatments like Erica Armstrong Dunbar's *She Came to Slay: The Life and Times of Harriet Tubman*, and the *Ms.* magazine Special Anniversary Issue conceived by the Black feminist historian Janell Hobson that featured work by Deirdre Cooper Owens (a historian of slavery and medicine currently writing a biography of Tubman focused on disability) and other Tubman experts, helped to round out the secondary biographical and historical literature that I consulted. Hobson herself is working on a comprehensive biography of Tubman, which will be a necessary and welcome addition to the literature. The original archival research represented here focuses on enslaved people's accounts of the Leonid meteor storm and reports about Tubman in Underground Railroad correspondence. Additionally, the Horton and Humez books noted above, as well as Bradford's early biography, include original documents as appendices. While I did not use it as a source, I reflected on the historian Elizabeth Cobbs's work of historical fiction, *The Tubman Command*, especially with regard to Tubman's baking and the uses of dialect by writers who focus on Tubman.[2] Importantly, I turned to the enlightening findings of state and national parks rangers and scholars, Tubman descendants interviewed for a Maryland State Parks oral history project (assisted by the oral history specialist at the Reginald F. Lewis Museum of Maryland African American History and Culture in Baltimore), Maryland state archaeologists, Harriet Tubman and William Henry Seward historic site guides, and Black female theologians to thicken and contextualize my study of Tubman, as well as to frame the stakes of her life story in the present moment.

The thematic focus of this book has been Tubman's worldview—meaning her religious faith, her thoughts and ideas, her environmental consciousness, and her holistic application of these aspects in life practice. The conceptual framework I selected echoes those emphases, enlisting feminist, theological, and ecological lenses. This has therefore been what might be called an ecowomanist telling of Harriet Tubman's life story. *Ecowomanism* derives from *womanism*, a body of thought and set of methods taken up by Black women theologians in the late 1990s and early 2000s. I adopted an ecowomanist approach for this project in part because it seems uniquely fitting for Tubman's own philosophical and phenomenological orientation and in part because it seems emphatically fitting for our times.

Harriet Tubman is claimed as a foremother of the Black women's spiritual and activist tradition known in church and divinity school circles as womanism, and likewise of ecowomanism, the ecologically attuned wing of this tradition concerned as much with justice for the earth as with justice for people (inseparable goals, in reality). Alice Walker first defined the term *womanism* in her short story "Coming Apart" (1979) and then with greater specificity in her book *In Search of Our Mothers' Gardens: Womanist Prose* (1983).[3] Walker introduced this neologism in order to name and delineate an African American and women of color feminist tradition that had arisen organically from Black culture. Drawing on Black folk practices and language, Walker's definition emphasized women's audaciousness, willfulness, and interdependence with men who were integral to families and could not be cast aside in the struggle for justice. Her characterization incorporated emotionality, spirituality, sexuality, and aesthetics through the language of "wholeness" and "health." Identifying as womanists and taking up this holistic outlook, Black women religious thinkers, led by the initial formulation of theologian Katie Cannon in 1998, developed theories of God, methods of biblical interpretation, and ethical principles drawing on Walker's articulation.[4] "Womanism" is today bound up with this spiritual ethos more tightly than "Black feminism," a theoretical sibling that entails a sharper political tone and often draws on critical analyses of the legacies of slavery and the specious foundations and operations of the U.S. state rather than on Christian themes like hope, forgiveness, and redemption.

Womanism bases a concept of freedom, dignity, and care for all in feminist interpretations of the Bible rooted in Black histories and cultural understandings. As a canonical thinker in this area of study, Delores Williams has explained, "Womanist theology assumes the necessity of responsible freedom for all human beings." Ecowomanism integrates the planet, environment, and natural world into this vision of democratic liberation, recognizing that violent harm done to Black women and women of color has often paralleled and interlocked with harm done to the earth. While tracing the spiritual path of Harriet Tubman's life, this book has shown her to be a person full of the Spirit, carrying consciousness of the earth, bearing witness for her God as she aided the people. I have also endeavored to respectfully reveal in these pages that as much as Tubman was sharp, wise, brave, and caring, she was also hurt, traumatized, and compromised. It is surely Harriet Tubman, a complex woman with gifts and scars, whom Alice Walker had in mind, and indeed memorialized, when she concluded her definition of *womanist* with the scenario of an enslaved daughter leading her mother and "a bunch of other slaves" to Canada. Womanist thinkers who took up Walker's neologism also highlighted Tubman, referring to her as a prophet of the Black women's religious tradition whose actions exemplified the "black church Godforce."[5]

As mentioned in the Introduction with a promise to follow up here, I first encountered womanist thought when I was a graduate student in Women's Studies in the early 1990s. Thirty years later, as environmental crises and anxieties have accelerated apace, I have noted a heightened attention to ecowomanism as a gradation of womanism fitted to the needs of our moment. On Earth Day 2017, I co-organized and cohosted an environmental retreat at the

University of Michigan in Ann Arbor under the auspices of the community program ECO Girls, which I had founded, and the BlackGirlLand Project, founded by the literary critic Tamara Butler, then at Michigan State University. The event, titled "Of Sea and Thunder and Spring: An Intellectual Retreat on Black Women and Environment," was co-conceived by the professional storyteller Elizabeth James, the aforementioned Butler, and me. Elizabeth James commented at that gathering: "[W]omen of color are synonymous with the land. We are responsible for making sure that people live somewhere and get fed. We are responsible for navigating the land to care for others . . . for nourishment of our communities . . . [But] we have a history of being displaced—from Africa, through Native land dispossession, through slave sales and gentrification." Recognizing that "the land is its own entity," she asked those present: "How do we care for the land under these circumstances, and how do we care for the people?" The group determined that one way to begin to answer these questions was by naming the philosophical orientation and mission, and a conversation ensued about terminology. Weighing the historical associations and connotations of *Black feminism*, *ecofeminism*, and *ecowomanism*, the group preferred the third term, not anticipating that Melanie Harris would soon release her treatise, part memoir, part analysis, titled *Ecowomanism: African American*

Women and Earth-Honoring Faiths (2017). A scholar of African American studies and religion, Melanie Harris has defined ecowomanism as an approach "influenced by the discipline of religion, and the discourse of spiritual ecology" that demonstrates "the theological voices and ethical perspectives from women of African descent as they contribute new strategies for facing climate change and promoting earth justice."[6] This is an approach with political undertones, summed up by Harris as "reveal[ing] the need for a fresh environmental justice paradigm; one that honors all earthlings and their approaches to earth justice in a community of life."[7] Leaning into this framework for my telling of Harriet Tubman's life of faith, thought, and practice, I have emphasized holistic understanding, Black women's lineages and traditions, the centrality of spirituality, the fight for racial justice, and a view of the earth as a living entity teeming with other alive things, all of which interact with the human quest for love and liberation.[8]

To begin the work of researching and narrating Harriet Tubman's story, I visited her original homeplace just months before the 2022 bicentennial anniversary celebration of her birth. In the fall of 2021, I traveled to Dorchester County, Maryland, where Tubman was born and enslaved for nearly thirty years. There, outside the town of Cambridge and in the small village of Bucktown, and on points along the country roads in between, a disjointed string of historic sites related to Tubman's early life remain intact. The Harriet Tubman Underground Railroad State Park Visitor Center stands in testament to her memory near a preserved nature area, the Blackwater National Wildlife Refuge. Guidebooks, pamphlets, websites, and signage encourage visitors to trace the roads that Tubman walked. I was eager to tread this ground. I rely on time spent in the places where certain events unfolded to help me reconstruct people and their past worlds, and I had expected that visiting the Eastern Shore of the Chesapeake Bay would supercharge a link to Tubman and anchor my sense of her life. I had timed the trip to Maryland for October, the same month when Tubman made her permanent escape from slavery in 1849, hoping that I might glean additional surety from seasonal cues and colors.

But things did not go as planned for that trip. I ended up traveling on the heels of the second big COVID-19 wave (Delta). While I was clicking my seat belt into place on the airplane, I received a message from my guide, Diane Miller, national program manager of the National Underground Railroad Network to Freedom of the National Park Service, whose office was at the Tubman State Park in Maryland. One of Dr. Miller's coworkers had contracted COVID, and she and her colleagues who had planned to guide me through Tubman sites (including the recently uncovered and reportedly impossible-to-find-unless-you-know-where-it-is Ben Ross cabin) were going into quarantine. I stared at the words on my phone screen, trying to determine if I should abort the trip, until I was forced to switch the device into airplane mode, the decision having been made by the random element of timing. As the jet nosed into the air, I knew I would be on my own navigating unfamiliar, partly unmarked terrain.

The Eastern Shore of Maryland along the Chesapeake Bay is still rural, still wet, with wide open, marshy fields bisected by creeks, rivulets, and stands of hardwood trees intermixed with pines. The bay is "the largest and most productive estuary" in the country, touching six states and numerous ancestral Indigenous territories with the edges of its brackish waters.[9] As I traveled in the rear seat of a taxi, I was struck by the feeling of continuity elicited by this deceptively timeless landscape, by the tiny towns and tired structures (dwellings as well as barns) that appeared as though they could have been built in the 1800s. I was fortunate to be staying at a hotel by the bay recommended by my quarantining colleague, and luckier to find a local driver recommended by the hotel clerk. He was an African American man who knew the location of Tubman's places and had an abundance of patience and kindness. He was willing to spend a day driving me down two-lane roads and waiting while I explored each site. I went first to the Tubman State Park, as much an environmental exhibit as it is an historical interpretive site. There I measured the height and traced the sway of the grasses with my admittedly untrained eye, walked to the border of the wildlife preserve and peered into the dense woods, looking for all indications of water—creeks, streams, swamps, marshes, the ruts of old canals, and the choppy surface of the Chesapeake Bay. But even as I stared into the dark waters, felt the cool autumn breeze, and listened to birdsong falling away into the dusk—even as I walked the borderline of property once owned by Tubman's enslavers and stood on the steps of the store where an overseer injured her—I could not gather to my chest a sense of the mighty woman herself. I had found Tubman's places, but not her.

This was a first for me—feeling thwarted in the hope of drawing closer to a historical figure by visiting their homeplace. Scholars and historic site interpreters disagree on how much the landscape where Tubman lived has changed over time, especially due to the gradual effects of climate change, which is making the region warmer and wetter.[10] An informal debate has emerged in National Park Service literature, popular literature, and scholarly literature about the extent to which Tubman's woods and waterways, the ones she sheltered by and waded through, still have the appearance and physical qualities she would have experienced, and why that should matter to us.[11] But my inability to touch Tubman by traveling to the place of her birth had less to do with the changing landscape stemming from climate and more to do with my own hubris, or perhaps it is kinder to say lack of imagination. Elizabeth James, a spiritual intuitive as well as a storyteller, told me as much when I admitted my frustration months after the visit.

"No one could catch her then," Beth said. "It's going to be hard to catch her now."

She was right, of course. Harriet Tubman was a master of flight. She had left coastal Maryland behind by choice. Why did I think I would find her there when no one else had? As I sat across the table from my insightful friend in an art museum café, my thoughts turned to Frederick Douglass's description of Tubman in the letter previously noted in the Conclusion of this book. A comrade in the struggle, Douglass had recognized Tubman's penchant for privacy. "Most that I have done and suffered for our cause has been in public," Douglass wrote. "You, on the other hand, have labored in a private way. I have wrought in the day—you in the night."[12] I realized I was chasing a woman of great spiritual power who in death, as in life, hid her secrets under night's wing. Still,

Beth urged me not to give up, but instead to loosen up, to try drawing nearer to Tubman by "holding her with tender hands . . . because we need her."

How do we tenderly hold an elusive woman like Harriet Tubman, a woman whose national memory has been weighted down by myth and lore? I think we begin by centering the things she held most dear—faith, family, and community. We continue by making room for her to speak for herself as much as possible, by respecting the boundaries she placed around her own feelings and secrets, and by trying our hardest to picture her before she knew—or we knew—who Harriet Tubman would become. My first aim in this book has been to humanize Harriet Tubman—to represent her in the fullness of her human multidimensionality to the extent that her imperfectly recorded words allow. My second aim has been to responsibly legacize Tubman (bending "legacy" into a verb), to show what she has bequeathed us in the realm of ideas, especially for her many intellectual descendants— womanists, feminists, tree huggers, freedom-lovers, shelter- makers, caretakers, and earth-walkers—while resisting her mythologization as a lone hero. I have tried to hold Harriet Tubman up—tenderly and honestly—in her genius, courage, vulnerability, faith, and flaws. And here at the end, I release her story back to the worldwide well of wise women, know- ing she will not tolerate our scrutiny for long.

Acknowledgments

Many generous people made this book possible, and I am grateful for all of them, named and unnamed. Tanya McKinnon, my agent, suggested that I try my hand at petite biography and chatted with me about how I saw Tubman's time in the woods. Editors Skip Gates and Scott Moyers embraced my concept and offered essential feedback on the project, making room for an early-nineteenth-century figure not often associated with philosophy, theory, or artistry in a biography series on Black thinkers and artists—and encouraging my environmental emphasis. I am grateful to the production editors, copy editors, and designers who stewarded the book through production at Penguin Press, particularly assistant editor Helen Rouner. Although she did not work on this book, I was channeling the gentle, sculpting approach of my Random House editor, Molly Turpin, as I revised.

Kate Larson warmly and enthusiastically supported my endeavor, going above and beyond my wildest wishes as an email correspondent, information sharer, and reader of the draft. She provided me not only with a cache of materials she had collected over the years and permission to use maps drawn for her own book but also with critical feedback and corrections as well as her latest thoughts on Tubman's youth and the Ben Ross site. Had it not been for Kate Larson's standout generosity, this book would surely have taken me twice as long to write. Everyone I encountered who was working on Tubman at the local level commented on how Kate Larson had assisted them. She is a model community-oriented scholar who genuinely wants to see Tubman's history advanced in as many ways, by as many people, as possible.

Catherine Clinton, my former professor, was a steady, encouraging presence as I worked on this book even though she didn't know I was writing it. She sent me cards and photos, came to hear me speak, and voiced her ongoing support of my path. When I was a college student at Harvard, Catherine Clinton taught the first course I had ever had the privilege of taking on Black women's history. She gave me my first research assistant job, too, introducing me to the Works Progress Administration (WPA) slave narratives (long before they were digitized) with the assignment to identify subject-specific passages on Black women. During a heavy summer of travel, she took time out to read my manuscript twice and offered feedback that added dimension. I owe much of my scholarly trajectory to her early influence, as well as the later support of my dear dissertation cochairs, David Roediger and Carol Miller, and dear committee members Jean O'Brien, Angela Dillard, and Brenda Child, then of the University of Minnesota. The storyteller and University of Michigan outreach coordinator Beth James has had a lasting influence on at least three of my books so far. She is a wise soul and generous conversation partner who enriches my ideas.

I have had the good fortune to work with wonderful graduate student and undergraduate student research assistants on this project. Dylan Nelson and Hannah Scruggs, both doctoral students at Harvard, have now worked with me on multiple projects. I trust them with my books, and that says everything. Perri Meldon, a graduate student at Boston University, has been integral to this research; she helped with research on the ground in Maryland and took a series of photos for me while she was researching Tubman's environments for her own dissertation on federal wildlife refuges (chiefly swamplands) as public history sites. I had the delight of working with several undergraduate students who conducted research for me under the auspices of Radcliffe and/or at the Schlesinger Library: Lucy Jackson, Orlee Marini-Rapoport, Kyra March, and Alejandro Eduarte; Lucy Jackson deserves an extra-special thanks for her long-term dedication to this project, abundant good cheer, and hands-on work with images, captions, proofreading, and permissions. Guiding Lucy Jackson as well as Josie Abugov on their senior theses while I was writing inspired renewed enthusiasm for my own project, and I am grateful to them both. Marjai Kamara, a then undergraduate student in environmental studies and Afroamerican and African Studies at the University of Michigan, was a key organizer of the Black feminist environmental retreat, a gathering that influenced my approach for this book.

Keen and empathetic public historians, writers, musicians, scholars, ministers, booksellers, friends, and family members all shared thoughts, knowingly or unknowingly, that strengthened this study. I am grateful to: Lauret Savoy, Melissa Bartholomew, Diane Miller, Dorceta Taylor, Edda Fields-Black, Dana Paterra, Barbara Tagger, Kelly Cunningham, Martha Jones, Angela Dillard, Kyera Singleton, Dan Smith, Sadada Jackson, Tayana Hardin, Sara St. Antoine, Frances Roberts-Gregory, Kerri Arsenault, Elizabeth Cobbs, Brian Klopotek, Jane Kamensky, Rebecca Walkowitz, Taylor Maurice, Tom Congalton, Manisha Sinha, Susan Kollin,

Mary Murphy, Ned Friedman, Mary Kelley, Emily Grogan, and Frances Smith Foster. Jeff Ludwig, director of education, and Kate Grindstaff, education and outreach coordinator, at the Seward House Museum generously offered their time and clarified my understanding of the Miller land inheritance and the Seward-Tubman land sale. Listeners at talks I gave on the Tubman research at the Harvard Radcliffe Institute (2022), at the Boston University Humanities Forum (2023), and at the University of Minnesota (2023) made insightful comments and asked expansive questions that improved this study. At Radcliffe, where I gave the first presentation on this material with fellows in our cohort year (2021–22), I received essential feedback from everyone present, particularly Scott Manning Stevens, Ariela Gross, Amy Farrell, Robin Mitchell, Anne Whiston Spirn, Elizabeth Baker, and Faren Humes. My fellow co-conveners (Jennifer Van Horn, Christine DeLucia, Scott Stevens) and the speakers at the "Objects, Pathways, and Afterlives" conference on material cultures at the Huntington Library (2023) helped to further my thinking about the materials of Tubman's life. Organizers Michelle Commander and Natasha Lightfoot and speakers at the "Slavery Archives and Affect" conference at the Schomburg Center (2023) inspired me as I pushed through to the end of this book's first draft, helping me to remember what our shared purpose is as Black women historians. As Celia Naylor said on the stage during our joint keynote dialogue: the purpose of our work is healing. And as Deedee Cooper said to me later that evening when we spoke alone of our adoration for our grandparents: "We do it for them."

I was able to carry out the site visits that were essential to this book because of kind taxi or rideshare drivers, all Black men, who insisted on staying with me, or coming back for me, in places where they thought I might need safe transport, especially Danny Seabrease of Breezeway Transportation in Cambridge, Maryland. I read and wrote many pages for *Night Flyer*, including these final lines, in the serene home of Clark Maher, owner of the 2 West Lake Bed & Breakfast in Skaneateles, New York, near Tubman's adopted hometown of Auburn. From Clark's front porch, I could view one of the Finger Lakes, the course of waterways where Tubman spoke with an interviewer on a veranda, also outside.

My extended family is the bedrock for all that I can accomplish; without them, I would be bewildered in this wide world. I am ever grateful to my parents, Patricia King and Benny Miles; to my stepparents, Montroue Miles and James King; to my siblings, Erin Miles and Erik Miles; and to the Banks, McCullom, Walker, Porter, Iron Shooter, Juelfs, Gone, and Azure families. To Joe Gone (my steadying spouse), Nali Gone and Noa Gone (my wonder twins), and Sylvan Gone (my baby beloved), thank you for making life shine.

Notes

PREFACE: THE STORM

1. Kate Clifford Larson, *Bound for the Promised Land: Harriet Tubman, Portrait of an American Hero* (2003; New York: One World, 2005), 358, 185. Sarah H. Bradford, *Harriet: The Moses of Her People* (G. R. Lockwood & Son, 1886; print to order via Amazon.com, 2011), 91. Alternate digital version: Smithsonian, https://library.si.edu/digital-library/book/harrietmosesofh00brad. The date of this storm given by Bradford may not be exact; it might have occurred in 1859 or 1860. (Note, the page numbers given for Bradford's texts throughout these notes are keyed to certain reprints as cited; the page numbers will not match those of the original editions, but all pages are discoverable in the originals through cross-referencing.)

2. Bradford, *Harriet* (1886), 7.

3. Ednah Dow Cheney, *Reminiscences* (Boston: Lee and Shephard, 1902), 81–82. Jean M. Humez, *Harriet Tubman: The Life and the Life Stories* (Madison: University of Wisconsin Press, 2003), 262,

415. This quote is attributed to a letter that Tubman dictated to be sent to Cheney in 1859, which appeared in Cheney's memoir. Collection Story "Harriet Tubman: Life, Liberty and Legacy," Smithsonian National Museum of African American History and Culture, https://nmaahc.si.edu/explore/stories/harriet-tubman.

4. Bradford, *Harriet* (1886), 91.

5. William Still, *The Underground Railroad* (1872), Toronto Metropolitan University Pressbooks, https://openlibrary-repo.ecampuson tario.ca/jspui/handle/123456789/1281. Accessed February 15, 2022.

6. Sarah H. Bradford, *Scenes in the Life of Harriet Tubman* (1869); *Some Additional Incidents in the Life of Harriet* (1901); and *Harriet: The Moses of Her People* (1886) compiled and reprinted as *The Extraordinary Life Story of Harriet Tubman* (e-artnow 2018), 102. (Note, the page numbers given for Bradford's texts throughout these notes are keyed to certain reprints as cited; the page numbers will not match those of the original editions, but all pages are discoverable in the originals through cross-referencing.)

7. Bradford, *Harriet* (1886), 38.

8. Delores S. Williams, *Sisters in the Wilderness: The Challenge of Womanist God-Talk* (Maryknoll, NY: Orbis Books, 1993), 6, 7, 188. Renita J. Weems, "Re-Reading for Liberation: African American Women and the Bible," in Katie Geneva Cannon, Emilie M. Townes, and Angela D. Sims, eds., *Womanist Theological Ethics: A Reader* (Louisville, KY: Westminster John Knox Press, 2011), 56.

9. Melissa Bartholomew, comment to Tiya Miles in a conversation on a bus, Mexico City, October 3, 2022. Quoted with permission.

10. David Crownson, *Harriet Tubman, Demon Slayer*, vol. 1, *America's Most Wanted* (New Jersey: Kingwood Comics, 2022). Kingwood Comics was created in 2020 by David Crownson. This independently published comic book was originally geared toward readers aged twelve to eighteen and developed a broader following.

NOTES

11. Bradford, *Harriet* (1886), 136.
12. Humez, *Harriet Tubman*, 290, 420. Emma P. Telford, "Harriet: The Modern Moses of Heroism and Visions" (1905), Cayuga Museum of History and Art, Auburn, New York, 13.
13. Humez, *Harriet Tubman*, 265.
14. Bradford, *Scenes* (1869), 27; Bradford, *Some Additional Incidents* (1901), 130.
15. Bradford, *Some Additional Incidents* (1901), 102.
16. W. E. Burghardt Du Bois, *John Brown* (Philadelphia: George W. Jacobs & Company, 1909), 249–50. Also consider Du Bois's comments about Tubman made in 1907, when he called her "a most remarkable black woman, unlettered and very negrine." Henry Louis Gates, Jr., ed., *100 Amazing Facts about the Negro* (New York: Pantheon Books, 2017), 67.
17. Tubman's humor: Judith Bryant interview, Oral History Project, "Tubman," Video Art Productions, Harriet Tubman Underground Railroad State Park Visitor Center (Maryland State Parks and Department of Economic Development), November 18, 2011, 7–18; Humez, *Harriet Tubman*, "Stories and Sayings," 256. Tubman's dresses/attire: Ednah Dow Cheney, "Moses," Freedmen's Bureau Records, March 1865, reprinted in Lois E. Horton, *Harriet Tubman and the Fight for Freedom: A Brief History with Documents* (Boston: Bedford/St. Martins, 2013), 138; Tubman to Franklin Sanborn, dictated letter, Humez, *Harriet Tubman*, 283–84; Humez, *Harriet Tubman*, "Stories and Sayings," 265. Tubman and fruit: Cheney, "Moses," 138; Humez, *Harriet Tubman*, "Stories and Sayings," 254.
18. Deirdre Cooper Owens, "Harriet Tubman's Disability and Why It Matters," *Ms.*, February 10, 2022, 3.
19. Bryant interview, Oral History Project, Maryland State Parks, 28. Bryant's great-great-grandfather was Tubman's brother. She de-

scribed her genealogical relationship to Tubman as follows: "Her brother is my great, great grandfather. That's the simple answer." Bryant interview, Oral History Project, Maryland State Parks, 2.

20. My offering of a new term for Tubman's life approach or practice, *luminous pragmatism*, was inspired by Dianne Glave's description of enslaved people's orientation to nature: "African Americans have long envisioned the environment in luminous and evocative ways, while at the same time remaining pragmatic and realistic about the wilderness." Dianne D. Glave, *Rooted in the Earth: Reclaiming the African American Environmental Heritage* (Chicago: Lawrence Hill Books, 2010), 6.

21. Bryant interview, Oral History Project, Maryland State Parks, 29.

INTRODUCTION: THE WAY

1. William L. Andrews, ed., *Sisters of the Spirit: Three Black Women's Autobiographies of the Nineteenth Century* (Bloomington: Indiana University Press, 1986). *Six Women's Slave Narratives*, "Introduction" by William L. Andrews, Schomburg Library of Nineteenth-Century Black Women Writers (New York: Oxford University Press, 1988).

2. Old Elizabeth, *Memoir of Old Elizabeth* (1863), in *Six Women's Slave Narratives*, title page.

3. Jarena Lee, *The Life and Religious Experience of Jarena Lee* (1836), in Andrews, ed., *Sisters of the Spirit*, 27, 47. Julia Foote, *A Brand Plucked from the Fire: An Autobiographical Sketch by Mrs. Julia A. J. Foote* (1879), in Andrews, ed., *Sisters of the Spirit*, 189.

4. Lee, *Life and Religious Experience*, 47.

5. Larson, *Bound for the Promised Land*, 49; also see 48–52.

6. Old Elizabeth, *Memoir*, 17.

NOTES

7. T. M. Luhrmann, *How God Becomes Real: Kindling the Presence of Invisible Others* (Princeton: Princeton University Press, 2020), xii, 22–25, 31–32; xi, 110, 113.

8. Emilie M. Townes, "Ethics as an Art of Doing the Work Our Souls Must Have," in Cannon, Townes, and Sims, *Womanist Theological Ethics*, 39.

9. Kimberly N. Ruffin, *Black on Earth: African American Ecoliterary Traditions* (Athens: University of Georgia Press, 2010), 2; Glave, *Rooted in the Earth*, 6.

10. Ruffin, *Black on Earth*, 72.

11. Crenshaw quote: Allison Keyes, "Harriet Tubman, an Unsung Naturalist, Used Owl Calls as a Signal on the Underground Railroad," *Audubon* magazine, February 25, 2020.

12. Perri Meldon, "Muck as Material Culture: Canals, Enslaved Labor, and Public History in the Mid-Atlantic," paper presented at conference on "Objects, Pathways, and Afterlives: Tracing Material Cultures in Early America," Huntington Library, San Marino, California, April 22, 2023.

13. Michael E. Ruane, "Harriet Tubman's Lost Maryland Home Found, Archaeologists Say," *Washington Post*, April 20, 2021.

14. Dorceta E. Taylor, *The Rise of the American Conservation Movement: Power, Privilege, and Environmental Protection* (Durham: Duke University Press, 2016), loc. 2636, Kindle. Chanda Prescod-Weinstein, "Harriet Tubman, Astronomer Extraordinaire," *Ms.*, February 3, 2022, 4.

15. Luhrmann, *How God Becomes Real*, xiii.

16. Aurélien de la Chapelle, Birgit Frauscher, Amandine Valomon, Perrine Marie Ruby, and Laure Peter-Derex, "Relationship between Epilepsy and Dreaming: Current Knowledge, Hypotheses, and Perspectives," *Frontiers in Neuroscience* 15 (2021): 2, 3, 4, 5. Ian Bone

and Simon Dein, "Religion, Spirituality, and Epilepsy," *Epilepsy & Behavior* 122 (2021): 1, 5, 6, 7, 8.

17. Toni Morrison, *Beloved* (New York: Plume, 1987), 87.

18. Morrison, *Beloved*, 87.

19. Sharony Green, *The Chase and Ruins: Zora Neale Hurston in Honduras* (Baltimore: Johns Hopkins University Press, 2023), xii.

20. Still, *Underground Railroad*, 487.

CHAPTER 1: THE WATER

1. In characterizing the young Tubman's experience, I borrow the concept and term of the "demon Slavery" from Harriet Jacobs's writing. Harriet A. Jacobs, *Incidents in the Life of a Slave Girl* (1861; Cambridge: Harvard University Press, 1987), 158.

2. The year 1822 is an estimate and will be used as a general time anchor in this book. The exact year of Harriet Tubman's birth is not known. Her gravestone in Auburn, New York, reads: "To the Memory of HARRIET TUBMAN DAVIS. Heroine of the Underground Railroad. Nurse and Scout in the Civil War. Born about 1820 in Maryland." Some historians and state and national parks officials have settled on the year 1822 as the likeliest date, based on evidence of payment to a midwife in that year, unearthed by Kate Larson. Jean Humez has suggested a date of 1820 or thereabouts, based on the written estimates of contemporaries Anthony C. Thompson and Franklin B. Sanborn. While acknowledging that 1820–22 tends to be the standard date range given, Catherine Clinton has put forward the year 1825, based on pension applications in which Tubman gave that date. It is possible that an 1838 Dorchester County court document, owned by a private citizen and yet to be authenticated, may provide more clues about Tubman's recorded age in that year

and hence about her estimated birth date. We may never know the exact date of Tubman's birth, and the debate itself is an instructive example of how historical researchers can gather and interpret evidence differently. Tubman gravestone, Fort Hill Cemetery, Auburn, New York. Larson, *Bound for the Promised Land*, xiv, 16; Humez, *Harriet Tubman*, 12, 354. Catherine Clinton, *Harriet Tubman: The Road to Freedom* (New York: Little, Brown, 2004), 4. Jacobs, *Incidents in the Life*, 158.

3. Maryland State Wildlife Action Plan 2015–25, 22, https://dnr .maryland.gov/wildlife/Pages/plants_wildlife/SWAP_home.aspx. Maryland at a Glance: Native Americans, https://msa.maryland .gov/msa/mdmanual/01glance/native/html/01native.html.

4. Larson, *Bound for the Promised Land*, 8. Clinton, *Harriet Tubman*, 5–6. For a moving description of Modesty's experience, see Erica Armstrong Dunbar, *She Came to Slay: The Life and Times of Harriet Tubman* (New York: 37 Ink, 2019), 5–7. In a search of the Slave Voyages Trans-Atlantic Slavery Database for arrivals into Maryland between 1770 and 1784, my research assistant, Lucy Jackson, found six ships, five of which originated in Saint-Louis, Senegal, and one of which originated in Gambia. The ships all arrived between 1770 and 1773, which reasonably corresponds with Modesty having a child, Rit, in the following decade, https://www.slavevoyages.org /voyage/database.

5. Larson, *Bound for the Promised Land*, 9. Kate Larson email to Tiya Miles, July 16, 2023.

6. Meteor: Maryland State Wildlife Action Plan, 8. Number of Green-Ross children: Horton, *Harriet Tubman*, 7; Kate Larson email to Tiya Miles, July 16, 2023. In this email, Larson lists the following individuals as children of Rit and Ben, with approximate birth years and approximate dates of sale:

Linah—1808 (sold between 1834 and 1844)
Mariah Ritty—1811 (aka Rhody, sold in 1825)
Soph—1813 (likely sold 1844)
Robert—1816 (free name, John Stewart, Sr.)
Araminta—1822 (aka Harriet Tubman)
Ben, Jr.—1823–24 (free name, James Stewart, Sr.)
Rachel—1825
Henry—1830 (freedom name, William Henry Stewart, Sr.)
Moses—1832

Details about the life of Tubman and her family have been growing over time as researchers dig further.

7. Larson, *Bound for the Promised Land*, 13. Clinton, *Harriet Tubman*, 9–10. Seth Rockman, *Scraping By: Wage Labor, Slavery, and Survival in Early Baltimore* (Baltimore: Johns Hopkins University Press, 2009), 13. For a discussion of the "off-loading" principle that hiring slaves out adhered to, see Dylan C. Penningroth, *Before the Movement: The Hidden History of Black Civil Rights* (New York: Liveright, 2023), 8–9.

8. Telford, "Harriet: Modern Moses," 3. Kate Larson kindly shared this transcription of Tubman's word *bode,* meaning "board," derived from her conversations with local residents; Kate Larson email to Tiya Miles, July 16, 2023.

9. Maryland Department of Planning, Jefferson Patterson Park and Museum, Education—Plants, https://jefpat.maryland.gov/Pages/education/plants/sweet-gum.aspx. Forest Service, U.S. Department of Agriculture, Research and Development, Southern Research Station, https://www.srs.fs.usda.gov/pubs/misc/ag_654/volume_2/liquidambar/styraciflua.htm.

10. Benjamin Drew, *The Narratives of Fugitive Slaves in Canada* (Bos-

ton: John P. Jewett and Company, 1856), 30. See also the 2008 paperback edition: Benjamin Drew, *The Refugee: Narratives of Fugitive Slaves in Canada* (Boston: Dundurn, 2008). For further analysis of Tubman's "neglected weed" quote, see Tiya Miles, *Wild Girls: How the Outdoors Shaped the Women Who Challenged a Nation* (New York: W. W. Norton, 2023), 13.

11. Larson, *Bound for the Promised Land*, 20.

12. Telford, "Harriet: Modern Moses," 3–4.

13. Telford, "Harriet: Modern Moses," 4.

14. Telford, "Harriet: Modern Moses," 4. Larson, *Bound for the Promised Land*, 37, 64. Clinton, *Harriet Tubman*, 19.

15. Bradford, *Harriet* (1886), 108. Telford, "Harriet: Modern Moses," 4. While Bradford says the Cook farm was ten miles away, Kate Larson has corrected that distance to being three miles to the west; Kate Larson email to Tiya Miles, July 16, 2023.

16. Telford, "Harriet: Modern Moses," 4.

17. Telford, "Harriet: Modern Moses," 4.

18. I am thankful to Perri Meldon, who shared her knowledge of muskrat trapping and the trade in pelts from her ongoing dissertation research on muskrat culture among diverse groups of people on Maryland's Eastern Shore.

19. Bradford, *Harriet* (1886), 109.

20. Bradford, *Harriet* (1886), 17. Larson, *Bound for the Promised Land*, 38.

21. Bradford, *Harriet* (1886), 17.

22. Elizabeth Keckley, *Behind the Scenes, or, Thirty Years a Slave, and Four Years in the White House* (1868; New York: Oxford University Press, 1988), 20–21.

23. Bradford, *Harriet* (1886), 18.

24. Bradford, *Some Additional Incidents* (1901), 101.

25. Bradford, *Scenes* (1869), 19–20.

26. Bradford, *Some Additional Incidents* (1901), 101.

27. Larson, *Bound for the Promised Land*, 40; Bradford, *Some Additional Incidents* (1901), 101–102. Telford, "Harriet: Modern Moses," 4.

28. Cheney, "Moses," 135.

CHAPTER 2: THE STARS

1. Old Elizabeth, *Memoir*, 3–4.

2. Zilpha Elaw, *Memoirs of the Life, Religious Experience, Ministerial Travels and Labours of Mrs. Zilpha Elaw* (1846), in Andrews, ed., *Sisters of the Spirit*, 7, 53, 58.

3. Also spelled Bazel's Church. "Bazel's Church," Maryland Historical Trust, Maryland Inventory of Historic Properties Form, Annapolis, Maryland. Larson, *Bound for the Promised Land*, 46.

4. Bradford, *Scenes* (1869), Appendix 57. Bradford, *Harriet* (1886), 71. Larson, *Bound for the Promised Land*, 45.

5. Katie Geneva Cannon, *Katie's Canon: Womanism and the Soul of the Black Community,* revised and expanded 25th Anniversary Edition (Minneapolis: Fortress Press, 2021), 77.

6. Andreas Brooks interview, Oral History Project, Maryland State Parks, October 24, 2011, 20.

7. "Photo Release: Governor Moore Announces Discovery of Home at Harriet Tubman Birthplace," Maryland Department of Transportation, February 13, 2023, https://www.mdot.maryland.gov/tso/pages/newsroomdetails.aspx?newsId=685&PageId=38. "Governor Wes Moore Announces Archaeological Discovery at Harriet Tubman's Birthplace," February 13, 2023, https://www.mdot.maryland.gov/tso/pages/newsroomdetails.aspx?newsId=684&PageId=38.

8. Bradford, *Harriet* (1886), 115, 69.

9. Larson, *Bound for the Promised Land*, 45.

10. Telford, "Harriet: Modern Moses," 4.

11. Bradford, *Harriet* (1886), 15–16.

12. Ursula Goodenough, *The Sacred Depths of Nature* (New York: Oxford University Press, 1998), xiv.

13. Foote, *A Brand Plucked*, 169, 175–76.

14. Larson posits that Tubman's witnessing of the sale of her sisters likely occurred in the 1830s; *Bound for the Promised Land*, 29, 32. Bradford, *Scenes* (1869), 20. A Dorchester County court document found by a private owner and yet to be authenticated appears to bear the date 1838 and includes names that would seem to support Larson's speculation as well as the notion that Tubman herself was being eyed for potential sale in this decade.

15. Swamp identification by Perri Meldon. Larson, *Bound for the Promised Land*, 32–33.

16. For enslaved people's memories of the Leonid meteor shower, see the WPA narratives, specifically: Lillie Baccus, WPA Slave Narratives, Arkansas, Part 1: 76, www.loc.gov/item/mesn021/. Rachel Bradley, WPA Slave Narratives, Arkansas, Part 1: 233, www.loc.gov /item/mesn021/. Elizabeth Brannon, WPA Slave Narratives, Arkansas, Part 1: 237. Peter Brown, WPA Slave Narratives, Arkansas, Part 1: 311, www.loc.gov/item/mesn021/. Betty Hodge, WPA Slave Narratives, Arkansas, Part 3: 282–83, www.loc.gov/item/mesn023/. Lizzie Johnson, WPA Slave Narratives, Arkansas, Part 4: 103, www.loc.gov/item/mesn024/. Lewis Evans, WPA Slave Narratives, South Carolina, Part 2: 30, www.loc.gov/item/mesn142/. Charlotte Foster, WPA Slave Narratives, South Carolina, Part 2: 83, www .loc.gov/item/mesn142/. Wesley Jones, WPA Slave Narratives, South Carolina, Part 3: 72, www.loc.gov/item/mesn143/. Gus Bradshaw, WPA Slave Narratives, Texas, Part 1: 130–31, www .loc.gov/item/mesn161/. Richard Caruthers, WPA Narratives, Texas, Part 1: 199. Willam Davis, WPA Slave Narratives, Texas, Part 1:

290, www.loc.gov/item/mesn161/. Also see "Jane Clark" by Julia C. Ferris, read at the banquet of the Cayuga County Historical Society, February 22, 1897. Also see Angela Y. Walton-Raji, "The Night the Stars Fell: My Search for Amanda Young," *My Ancestor's Name* (blog), https://myancestorsname.blogspot.com/2010/04/night-stars-fell-my-search-for-amanda.html. For a more detailed discussion of these memories of the meteor shower, see Miles, *Wild Girls*, 23–27.

17. Candace Greene, "Preface," Candace S. Greene and Russell Thornton, eds., *The Year the Stars Fell: Lakota Winter Counts at the Smithsonian* (Washington, DC: Smithsonian National Museum of Natural History, 2007), vi, viii. Greene and Thornton, eds., *Year the Stars Fell*, 584–85. Scientists estimate the number of stars in motion that evening at between 50,000 and 150,000. Mary L. Kwas, "The Spectacular 1833 Leonid Meteor Storm: The View from Arkansas," *Arkansas Historical Quarterly* 58, no. 3 (Autumn 1999): 314–24, 314, 316, 320. Eleanor Imster and Deborah Byrd, "The Night the Stars Fell," EarthSky.org, November 16, 2018, https://earthsky.org/todays-image/leonid-meteor-shower-1833. Various Lakota bands have produced the highest number and most studied winter counts; other nations, like the Kiowas and Blackfeet, also produced counts that have been preserved. Matthew D. Therrell and Makayla J. Trotter, "Waniyetu Wówapi: Native American Records of Weather and Climate," *Bulletin of the American Meteorological Society*, May 2011: 583–92.

18. For further analysis of the Harriet Powers Pictorial Quilt, see Tiya Miles, *All That She Carried: The Journey of Ashley's Sack, a Black Family Keepsake* (New York: Random House, 2021), 37–39.

19. "Aunt Harriet Was Very Old," *Auburn Daily Advertiser*, Auburn, New York, March 12, 1913. Kate Larson discusses this passage as

well as other Marylanders' reactions to the meteor shower; Larson, *Bound for the Promised Land*, 41.

20. Bradford, *Harriet* (1886), 109. Telford, "Harriet: Modern Moses," 5. Larson, *Bound for the Promised Land*, 42, 316.

21. Telford, "Harriet: Modern Moses," 4.

22. Bradford, *Scenes* (1869), 20. Larson, *Bound for the Promised Land*, 43. Owens, "Harriet Tubman's Disability," 5.

23. Owens, "Harriet Tubman's Disability," 5.

24. Telford, "Harriet: Modern Moses," 6–7.

25. Foote, *A Brand Plucked*, 180.

26. Old Elizabeth, *Memoir*, 5–7.

27. Elaw, *Memoirs of the Life*, 55–57.

28. Foote, *A Brand Plucked*, 180.

29. Andrews, "Introduction," *Sisters of the Spirit*, 12–13.

CHAPTER 3: THE WILDERNESS

1. Williams, *Sisters in the Wilderness*, 108–13, 117.

2. Telford, "Harriet: Modern Moses," 5.

3. Telford, "Harriet: Modern Moses," 6. Bradford, *Harriet* (1886), 22.

4. Rockman, *Scraping By*, 13. Distance calculated with Google Maps.

5. Drew, *Fugitive Slaves in Canada*, 30.

6. Bradford, *Harriet* (1886), 110. Bradford represents this unnamed white man as being the son of Tubman's guardian. Larson explains that it was likely Dr. Anthony C. Thompson, the son of Ben Ross's former owner, who vouched for Tubman. (Ross was Tubman's father.) Larson, *Bound for the Promised Land*, 64.

7. Larson, *Bound for the Promised Land*, 56.

8. Larson, *Bound for the Promised Land*, 56.

9. Janell Hobson, "Karen V. Hill, Director of the Harriet Tubman

Home: 'She Was Able to Separate the Brutality of Slavery from How She Loved the Land,'" *Ms.*, March 2, 2022: 3.

10. Glave, *Rooted in the Earth*, 6.

11. Cheney, "Moses," 135.

12. Catherine Clinton, *Harriet Tubman: The Road to Freedom* (New York: Little, Brown, 2004), 20.

13. Larson, *Bound for the Promised Land*, 59–60. Meldon, conference paper, "Muck as Material Culture."

14. Larson, *Bound for the Promised Land*, 58. Based on research in family documents, Larson notes that Ross and two other enslaved individuals (Jerry and Polly Manokey) received special treatment in the Thompson will, 69. Will of Anthony Thompson and Inventory of Enslaved Population, 1836, Dorchester County (Thompson Will 1–7).

15. Larson, *Bound for the Promised Land*, 58. Ruane, "Harriet Tubman's Lost Maryland Home." Kate Larson email exchange with Tiya Miles, July 16, 2023.

16. Bradford, *Harriet* (1886), 111.

17. Taylor, *Rise of the American Conservation Movement*, loc. 2677, Kindle. Ruane, "Harriet Tubman's Lost Maryland Home."

18. Bradford, *Harriet* (1886), 110. Penningroth, *Before the Movement*, 4.

19. Telford, "Harriet: Modern Moses," 6.

20. Luhrmann, *How God Becomes Real*, 112–13.

21. Old Elizabeth, *Memoir*, 5. Elaw, *Memoirs of the Life*, 67, 70, 71.

22. Foote, *A Brand Plucked*, 182, 186–87.

23. Lee, *Life and Religious Experience*, 30–31, 33, 40–42.

24. Lee, *Life and Religious Experience*, 40. Foote, *A Brand Plucked*, 186.

25. Bradford, *Harriet* (1886), 5.

26. Lee, *Life and Religious Experience*, 48.

NOTES

CHAPTER 4: THE DREAMS

1. Cheney, "Moses," 134. Larson, *Bound for the Promised Land*, 62.
2. Larson, *Bound for the Promised Land*, 62, 63. Clinton, *Harriet Tubman*, 27–28, 30.
3. Cheney, "Moses," 135.
4. Telford, "Harriet: Modern Moses," 7.
5. Bradford, *Scenes* (1869), 20.
6. Old Elizabeth, *Memoir*, 5, 6.
7. Bradford, *Scenes* (1869), 20.
8. Foote, *A Brand Plucked*, 186, 196. Elaw, *Memoirs of the Life*, 61, 63.
9. Bradford, *Harriet* (1886), 114–15.
10. Maryland State Wildlife Action Plan, 3.
11. Drew, *Fugitive Slaves in Canada*, 30.
12. Old Elizabeth, *Memoir*, 13. Elaw, *Memoirs of the Life*, 59. The memoirists are drawing on the Bible verse Jeremiah 12:9.
13. U.S. Fish & Wildlife Service, Blackwater Wildlife National Refuge, https://www.fws.gov/refuge/blackwater.
14. Scholars Dana Paterra (director of the Harriet Tubman Underground Railroad State Park and Visitor Center) and Diane Miller (director of the National Park Service Network to Freedom program) speculated that the egret was the most likely bird for Tubman to have pictured in her dreams. My research assistant, Perri Meldon, asked them this question on my behalf on April 13, 2022, at the Harriet Tubman Underground Railroad State Park Visitor Center.
15. Alexis Wells-Oghoghomeh, *The Souls of Womenfolk: The Religious Cultures of Enslaved Women in the Lower South* (Chapel Hill: University of North Carolina Press, 2021), 164. The female society Wells-Oghoghomeh names was Sande.
16. Larson, *Bound for the Promised Land*, 72. Calculated with West Egg online inflation calculator, figure $50, years 1848 and 2022.

NOTES

17. Bradford, *Harriet* (1886), 24.

18. Telford, "Harriet: Modern Moses," 7–8.

19. Larson, *Bound for the Promised Land*, 73. Telford, "Harriet: Modern Moses," 6–8.

20. Bradford, *Harriet* (1886), 24–25.

21. Andrews, "Introduction," *Sisters of the Spirit*, 13, 15.

22. Lee, *Life and Religious Experience*, 31, 33.

23. Larson, *Bound for the Promised Land*, 73–74, 76–77.

24. Larson, *Bound for the Promised Land*, 78. Clinton, *Harriet Tubman*, 34. The details and time sequence of this first escape attempt are not entirely clear in the record. The newspaper advertisement for the recapture of the siblings refers to one brother as Harry; however, Kate Larson has determined through cross-checking other primary sources that this brother was actually Henry.

25. Bradford, *Harriet* (1886), 27.

26. Telford, "Harriet: Modern Moses," 8.

27. Helen C. Rountree and Thomas E. Davidson, *Eastern Shore Indians of Virginia and Maryland* (Charlottesville: University of Virginia Press, 1997), Appendix C: Major Useful Wild Plants of the Eastern Shore of Maryland and Virginia, VIII. Pine Woods, 247.

28. Larson, *Bound for the Promised Land*, 79. Clinton, *Harriet Tubman*, 34.

29. Maryland State Wildlife Action Plan, 15.

30. Maryland State Wildlife Action Plan, 15. Sinisa Vujinovic, "Maryland Wild Side: Exploring Fascinating Native Wildlife," *Southwest Journal*, April 18, 2023, https://www.southwestjournal.com/maryland-wild-side/. "Chesapeake Wildlife," Chesapeake Bay Foundation, https://www.cbf.org/about-the-bay/chesapeake-wildlife/index.html.

31. Anne Whiston Spirn, *The Language of Landscape* (New Haven: Yale University Press, 1998), 19.

278

32. Maryland State Wildlife Action Plan, 4.

33. Spirn, *Language of Landscape*, 18.

34. Loren S. Cahill, "BlackGirl Geography: A (Re)Mapping Guide towards Harriet Tubman and Beyond," *Girlhood Studies* 12, no. 3 (Winter 2019): 47–62, 50.

35. Cheney, "Moses," 137.

CHAPTER 5: THE FLIGHT

1. Bradford, *Scenes* (1869), 22, 24. Bradford, *Harriet* (1886), 37.

2. Telford, "Harriet: Modern Moses," 8.

3. Jacqueline L. Tobin and Raymond G. Dobard, *Hidden in Plain View: A Secret Story of Quilts and the Underground Railroad* (New York: Doubleday, 1999).

4. Teri Klassen, "Representations of African American Quiltmaking: From Omission to High Art," *Journal of American Folklore* 122, no. 485 (Summer 2009): 319.

5. Klassen, "Representations of African American Quiltmaking," 297–334, 318, 319.

6. Klassen, "Representations of African American Quiltmaking," 318, 319. Robin Bernstein, *Racial Innocence: Performing American Childhood from Slavery to Civil Rights* (New York: New York University Press, 2011), 83, 84.

7. *Fabric of a Nation* exhibition, MFA Boston, https://www.mfa.org /exhibition/fabric-of-a-nation. Lisa Betty, "General Harriet Tubman (1820–1913): Healing Historical Exploitation," *Medium*, July 24, 2020, https://lbetty1.medium.com/general-harriet-tubman -1820-1913-healing-historical-exploitation-5e301a96b053.

8. Clinton, *Harriet Tubman*, 35. Larson, *Bound for the Promised Land*, 80. Humez, *Harriet Tubman*, 16–18.

9. Clinton, *Harriet Tubman*, 35.

10. Cheney, "Moses," 137.

11. For more on textiles as goods that women on the margins of society could use for exchange and trade as currency, see Laura F. Edwards, *Only the Clothes on Her Back: Clothing and the Hidden History of Power in the 19th-Century United States* (New York: Oxford University Press, 2022).

12. Larson, *Bound for the Promised Land*, 81–83. Clinton, *Harriet Tubman*, 35–36.

13. Clinton, *Harriet Tubman*, 37. Larson, *Bound for the Promised Land*, 80–84. Kate Larson email to Tiya Miles, July 16, 2023.

14. Larson, *Bound for the Promised Land*, 85.

15. Robert Pogue Harrison, *Forests: The Shadow of Civilization* (Chicago: University of Chicago Press, 1992), 76–77.

16. Alice Walker, *In Search of Our Mothers' Gardens: Womanist Prose* (New York: Harcourt Brace Jovanovich, 1983), xi.

17. Williams, *Sisters in the Wilderness*, 2, 3, 5, 121. *How Edmonia Lewis Became an Artist* (Albany? ca. 1870), Houghton Library, Harvard University, https://curiosity.lib.harvard.edu/slavery-abolition-emancipation-and-freedom/catalog/74-990057789120203941. "Edmonia Lewis, the Colored Sculptor at Chicago," *New York Times*, September 11, 1870.

18. Distance and time calculated with Google Maps. Quraysh Ali Lansana, *They Shall Run: Harriet Tubman Poems* (Chicago: Third World Press, 2004), 14.

19. Maryland State Wildlife Action Plan, 12.

20. Bradford, *Harriet* (1886), 30.

21. Bradford, *Harriet* (1886), 31–32.

22. Jacobs, *Incidents in the Life*, 158.

23. Bradford, *Harriet* (1886), 32.

24. Lansana, *They Shall Run*, 38.

25. Manisha Sinha, *The Slave's Cause: A History of Abolition* (New Haven: Yale University Press, 2016), 20–22, 238, 387.
26. Bradford, *Harriet* (1886), 44–45.
27. Bradford, *Scenes* (1869), 22.
28. Cheney, "Moses," 136.
29. Still, *Underground Railroad*, 884.
30. Larson, *Bound for the Promised Land*, 91.
31. Larson, *Bound for the Promised Land*, 89–90. Kessiah was the daughter of Linah, one of Tubman's two sisters sold by Brodess. Larson, *Bound for the Promised Land*, 32, 76.
32. Horton, *Harriet Tubman*, 24.
33. Larson, *Bound for the Promised Land*, 90. Clinton, *Harriet Tubman*, 82. Cheney, "Moses," 136.
34. Old Elizabeth, *Memoir*, 16. Lee, *Life and Religious Experience*, 41–42.
35. Elaw, *Memoirs of the Life*, 84–86, 90, 51. Andrews, "Introduction," *Sisters of the Spirit*, 8.
36. Andrews, "Introduction," *Sisters of the Spirit*, 9, 10. Foote, *A Brand Plucked*, 227.
37. Bradford, *Scenes* (1869), 23.
38. Harriet Tubman Underground Railroad Routes, Siebert Papers, Ohio Historical Society, https://ohiomemory.org/digital/collection/siebert/id/26822. Still, *Underground Railroad*, 405, 487. Bradford, *Harriet* (1886), 57. Kate Larson notes that the "cousin Tom" mentioned in this quotation from Siebert's records was Tubman's brother-in-law, Tom Tubman, who lived in Baltimore. Kate Larson email to Tiya Miles, July 16, 2023.
39. Bradford, *Harriet* (1886), 47, 50, 51.
40. Bradford, *Harriet* (1886), 36.
41. Still, *Underground Railroad*, 487.
42. Horton, *Harriet Tubman*, 27. Larson, *Bound for the Promised Land*,

xvii. Clinton, *Harriet Tubman*, 73. Due to gaps in the historical record, it is impossible to precisely count the number of men, women, and children Tubman rescued. While Bradford claimed as many as 300, Thomas Garrett posited 60 to 80 (Bradford, *Scenes* (1869), 31). Twenty-first-century historians who have examined extant accounts of the escapes estimate between 60 and 80 people directly aided through Tubman's physical guidance and around 50 to 60 people indirectly aided through information Tubman shared (Larson, *Bound for the Promised Land*, 100; Horton, *Harriet Tubman*, 27). The exhibit at the Harriet Tubman Underground Railroad State Park Visitor Center in Maryland includes a three-part panel titled "We are free because of Harriet Tubman," which lists each person saved by Tubman by name if that detail is known, describes unnamed people she aided, and notes people who were able to escape based on information she shared. This number does not include those rescued (around 700 to 750, firsthand accounts vary) during the Combahee River Raid of the Civil War.

43. Bradford, *Scenes* (1869), 24.
44. Larson, *Bound for the Promised Land*, 96. Douglass quoted in Philip S. Foner, ed., *The Life and Writings of Frederick Douglass*, vol. 2, *Pre-Civil War Decade* (New York: International Publishers, 1950), 46–47; also see Humez, *Harriet Tubman*, 30, 418. Cheney, "Moses," 136.
45. Telford, "Harriet: Modern Moses," 8.
46. Larson, *Bound for the Promised Land*, 111.
47. Larson, *Bound for the Promised Land*, 113. Still, *Underground Railroad*, 405.
48. Bradford, *Harriet* (1886), 114.
49. Larson, *Bound for the Promised Land*, 125–26.
50. Drew, *Fugitive Slaves in Canada*, 30.
51. Runaway advertisement for Tubman and brothers, *Cambridge Dem-*

ocrat, Cambridge, MD, October 3, 1849. Larson, *Bound for the Promised Land,* 100.

52. Bradford, *Scenes* (1869), 22. Du Bois, *John Brown,* 249–50. For a discussion of the reward issue, see Horton, *Harriet Tubman,* 24; Larson's view is that the reward amounts in the high thousands in the early record are unsubstantiated and may have been invented by the authors; Kate Larson email to Tiya Miles, July 16, 2023.

53. Bradford, *Scenes* (1869), 22.

54. Thomas Garrett reprinted in Bradford, *Scenes* (1869), 31.

55. Bradford, *Harriet* (1886), 81, 86.

56. Still, *Underground Railroad,* 884.

57. Telford, "Harriet: Modern Moses," 10, 11.

58. Bradford, *Harriet* (1886), 59–60. This account of Tilly's rescue differs in early sources, with Sarah Bradford offering a more dramatic chronicle than Thomas Garrett, both of whom heard the story from Tubman herself. My summary follows Kate Larson's lead in privileging Garrett's account and toning down the sensationalism and drama evident in Bradford's. Larson, *Bound for the Promised Land,* 131–33. Kate Larson email to Tiya Miles, July 16, 2023. Larson reads Tubman's numerical reference to seven as indicating that this was Tubman's seventh trip. This is sound reasoning, but I have chosen to abstract and enlarge Tubman's "seventh trouble" phrasing in this book for greater symbolic application to repeated crises.

59. Bradford, *Harriet* (1886), 55–56.

60. Telford, "Harriet: Modern Moses," 12.

61. Bradford, *Harriet* (1886), 73–74.

62. Telford, "Harriet: Modern Moses," 11.

63. Bradford, *Harriet* (1886), 61.

64. Telford, "Harriet: Modern Moses," 9.

65. Telford, "Harriet: Modern Moses," 10.

66. Bradford, *Harriet* (1886), 41–42.

67. Cheney, "Moses," 137.

68. Bradford, *Scenes* (1869), 23. Kellie Carter Jackson, *Force and Freedom: Black Abolitionists and the Politics of Violence* (Philadelphia: University of Pennsylvania Press, 2019), 8.

69. Garrett reprinted in Bradford, *Scenes* (1869), 31.

CHAPTER 6: THE DELIVERER

1. Humez, *Harriet Tubman*, 133.

2. Humez, *Harriet Tubman*, 6.

3. Bradford, *Some Additional Incidents* (1901), 105.

4. Humez, *Harriet Tubman*, 133.

5. Bradford, *Scenes* (1869), 22.

6. Frederick Douglass quoted in Humez, *Harriet Tubman*, 30.

7. Jacqueline Jones, *No Right to an Honest Living: The Struggles of Boston's Black Workers in the Civil War Era* (New York: Basic Books, 2023), 180.

8. Humez, *Harriet Tubman*, 42. Humez suggests that Tubman may have also been the model for a Black character in Louisa May Alcott's novel *Work*; 364, note 64, 65.

9. Cheney, "Moses," 138.

10. Dorothy Wickenden, *The Agitators: Three Friends Who Fought for Abolition and Women's Rights* (New York: Scribner, 2021), 137–39. Wickenden's research updates previous understandings that William H. Seward (senior) sold the house to Harriet Tubman. It seems, rather, that the home sale was Frances Seward's brainchild carried out by her son, with her husband's assent. Administrators at the William Seward House agree with this updated, more nuanced interpretation as of May 2023. See also Larson, *Bound for the Prom-*

ised Land, 163–65. Frances Seward and her sister inherited Elijah Miller's estate, while William H. Seward was the executor with legal control over the estate, https://sewardhouse.org/history/seward -house. Letter from William Henry Seward, Jr., to William Henry Seward, August 15, 1859, Seward Family Digital Archive, River Campus Libraries, University of Rochester, sewardproject.org. Larson, *Bound for the Promised Land*, 163. Jeff Ludwig, Director of Education, Seward House Museum, conversation with Tiya Miles, May 30, 2023.

11. Jeff Ludwig, conversation with Tiya Miles, May 30, 2023.

12. Letter from William Henry Seward, Jr., to William Henry Seward, August 15, 1859, Seward Family Digital Archive, River Campus Libraries, University of Rochester, sewardproject.org.

13. Calculations via the West Egg online inflation calculator, for the years 1859 and 2022.

14. Penningroth, *Beyond the Movement*, 79.

15. Michael Leroy Oberg, *Peacemakers: The Iroquois, The United States, and the Treaty of Canandaigua, 1794* (New York: Oxford University Press, 2016), 29, 91, 139.

16. Jeff Ludwig, conversation with Tiya Miles about the Miller and Seward land acquisitions and transfers, May 30, 2023. I am grateful to Jeff Ludwig, director of education, and Kate Grindstaff, education and outreach coordinator, at the Seward House Museum for these specifics about Miller and Seward family histories.

17. An additional complication and tension related to Tubman's home purchase in Auburn is the city's reliance on an infamously inhumane prison for its economic stability and growth. As the historian Robin Bernstein demonstrates, many Auburn residents derived their wealth, livelihoods, or political influence from ties to the Auburn State Prison, which forced inmates to perform uncompensated work and encouraged prison tourism. For Bernstein's

discussion of Tubman in Auburn and Tubman's single known mention of the prison, see Robin Bernstein, *Freeman's Challenge: The Murder That Shook America's Original Prison for Profit* (Chicago: University of Chicago Press, 2024), 181–84.

18. John Brown as quoted by Wendell Phillips, 1868, in Horton, *Harriet Tubman*, 143.

19. Bradford, *Harriet* (1886), 118.

20. Larson, *Bound for the Promised Land*, 173.

21. Larson, *Bound for the Promised Land*, 175.

22. Bradford, *Harriet* (1886), 117.

23. Bradford, *Harriet* (1886), 92.

24. This aspect of Tubman's life remains confusing and unsettling. According to the memory of Margaret Stewart's daughter, Alice Lucas Brickler, Harriet Tubman engaged in a "kidnapping" of Stewart, that is, taking the child away from Maryland without the foreknowledge or permission of her parents or guardians. There has been serious speculation in the historical literature that Margaret Stewart may have been Harriet Tubman's own daughter whom Harriet asked a relative to raise in her absence. This is a sensitive topic rife with complications, with Catherine Clinton holding the view that Tubman did have a daughter. She notes that Stewart was born around 1850, the same tumultuous period as Tubman's escape, and that Tubman, like some other Black women who moved by necessity, probably left her child in the care of others for strategic reasons. (Catherine Clinton, conversation with Tiya Miles, August 15, 2023.) Margaret Stewart, whose lighter skin was remarked upon by her daughter Alice, may have been fathered by a man other than John Tubman, Clinton has speculated in her book, linking this possibility to John Tubman's refusal to go north with Tubman in 1849. Kate Larson offers the tentative, though detailed, speculation that Tubman could have given birth

before her escape, or afterward in Baltimore, where she was present in December 1850 while trying to aid her niece Kessiah; Larson notes that Tubman could have then placed the baby in a relative's or friend's household. I will add the small link that Sarah Bradford wrote that Tubman was ill around December–March, just prior to Edward Brodess's death in March 1849 and about six months before she ran away. Could this sickness have been related to a pregnancy? Could Tubman have given birth around August or September 1849, only a month before her escape? Some Tubman descendants, including Alice Lucas Brickler citing her mother, have called Margaret Stewart a niece, at the same time other descendants have claimed that Margaret Stewart had no blood relationship to Tubman. These claims may reflect accurate group recollections or conflicting familial investments in particular narratives of kinship. When Tubman first brought Stewart to Auburn, New York, she placed the child with Lazette Worden, a sister of Frances Seward who lived with Frances through most of the Civil War. A relatively recent and detailed exhibition at the Seward House Museum describes Margaret Stewart Lucas's life and her murky relationship with Tubman based on family accounts and photographs. See "Convergence: Margaret Stewart and Bonds Deeper than Freedom," Seward House Museum, Auburn, New York. Humez, *Harriet Tubman*, 47. Clinton, *Harriet Tubman*, 117–23. Larson, *Bound for the Promised Land*, 196–202; also see photo insert, 5. Wickenden, *The Agitators*, 196. Note that Clinton's and Larson's books include pages of discussion on this issue (cited above).

25. Bradford, *Harriet* (1886), 140–42.
26. Telford, "Harriet: Modern Moses," 15–16. Bradford, *Harriet* (1886), 97–98. Humez, *Harriet Tubman*, 50, 52, 55–56.
27. Humez, *Harriet Tubman*, 61–63.

28. Bradford, *Harriet* (1886), 95. Bradford, *Scenes* (1869), 28. Cheney, "Moses," 139.

29. Cheney, "Moses," 139. Bradford, *Harriet* (1886), 97.

30. Jeff W. Grigg, *The Combahee River Raid: Harriet Tubman and Low-country Liberation* (Charleston, SC: History Press Library Editions, 2014), 13, 23–24. Clinton, *Harriet Tubman*, 164; Clinton names the band members as: Mott Blake, Peter Burns, Gabriel Cahern, George Chisholm, Isaac Hayward, Walter Plowden, Charles Simmons, and Sandy Suffus. Larson, *Bound for the Promised Land*, 210; Larson notes that eight of these men were local self-liberators and one was from New York; Kate Larson email to Tiya Miles, July 16, 2023. For more on Tubman in the war, see Earl Conrad, "I Bring You General Tubman," *The Black Scholar* 1, nos. 3–4 (1970).

31. Clinton, *Harriet Tubman*, 165.

32. Grigg, *Combahee River Raid*, 25, 28, 87–88.

33. Grigg, *Combahee River Raid*, 60–62.

34. Clinton, *Harriet Tubman*, 165.

35. Grigg, *Combahee River Raid*, 70–71.

36. Bradford, *Harriet* (1886), 100–101.

37. Bradford, *Harriet* (1886), 102. The hymn "Come Along, Come Along" was performed by the Hutchinson singers in the North; Kate Larson email to Tiya Miles, July 16, 2023. Different versions of this song were recorded in early sources; for a discussion of these variations, see Larson, *Bound for the Promised Land*, 366, note 71. Larson, *Bound for the Promised Land*, 303.

38. Grigg, *Combahee River Raid*, 79, 83.

39. Grigg, *Combahee River Raid*, 79, 83. James Yerrington, "Col. Montgomery's Raid," June 6, 1863 (June 20, 1863), *The State Journal*, https://access-newspaperarchive-com.ezp-prod1.hul.harvard.edu/us/wisconsin/madison/madison-wisconsin-state-journal/1863/06-20/page-2/; "From Florida: Colonel Montgomery's Raid,"

(Madison) Wisconsin State Journal, June 20, 1863, excerpted in Humez, *Harriet Tubman*, 60, 299–300.

40. Tubman dictated letter to Franklin Sanborn about the Combahee River Raid (1863), in Humez, *Harriet Tubman*, 283–84.

41. Cheney, "Moses," 138.

42. Tubman dictated letter to Sanborn, in Humez, *Harriet Tubman*, 283.

43. Tubman dictated letter to Sanborn, in Humez, *Harriet Tubman*, 283. Samuel J. May, *Some Recollections of Our Antislavery Conflict* (Boston: Fields, Osgood, 1869), quoted in Humez, *Harriet Tubman*, 249.

44. Edda L. Fields-Black, *Combee: Harriet Tubman, the Combahee River Raid, and Black Freedom during the Civil War* (New York: Oxford University Press, forthcoming February 2024).

45. W. E. B. Du Bois, *Black Reconstruction in America 1860–1880* (New York: Atheneum Books for Young Readers, 1992), 30.

46. Tubman dictated letter to Franklin Sanborn about the Combahee River Raid (1863), in Humez, *Harriet Tubman*, 283–84.

CHAPTER 7: THE CARETAKER

1. Cheney, "Moses," 138.

2. Bradford, *Harriet* (1886), 97.

3. Bradford cites this periodical as *The Evangelist*. Bradford, *Some Additional Incidents* (1901), 102. For more on the history of Fort Wrangell School, see Zachary R. Jones, "Yánde gaxhyinaakh aa kákh / You Will Stand Up to It: Indigenous Action in Southeast Alaska Native Education, 1878–1945," *Pacific Northwest Quarterly* 106, no. 1 (winter 2014–15): 3–15. Ted C. Hinckley, "The Early Alaskan Ministry of S. Hall Young, 1878–1888," *Journal of Presbyterian History* 46, no. 3 (September 1968): 175–96.

4. Elizabeth B. Chace to Wilbur Henry Siebert, November 4, 1893, Wilbur Henry Siebert Papers, Ohio Historical Society, https://ohiomemory.org/digital/collection/siebert/id/24408. Bradford, *Some Additional Incidents* (1901), 102.

5. Telford, "Harriet: Modern Moses," 20.

6. Cheney, "Moses," 138.

7. Larson, *Bound for the Promised Land*, 255–58. Humez, *Harriet Tubman*, 88–90. Clinton, *Harriet Tubman*, 201–202.

8. Foote, *A Brand Plucked*, 225. Old Elizabeth, *Memoir*, 19.

9. Telford, "Harriet: Modern Moses," 21.

10. Telford, "Harriet: Modern Moses," 23.

11. Larson, *Bound for the Promised Land*, 273.

12. Telford, "Harriet: Modern Moses," 22, 23. Bradford, *Some Additional Incidents* (1901), 105.

13. Williams, *Sisters in the Wilderness*, 175.

14. Williams, *Sisters in the Wilderness*, 175.

15. Elaw, *Memoirs of the Life*, 160. Old Elizabeth, *Memoir*, 19.

16. Bradford, *Some Additional Incidents* (1901), 102. Telford, "Harriet: Modern Moses," 20.

17. Bryant interview, Oral History Project, Maryland State Parks, 18.

18. Larson, *Bound for the Promised Land*, 74.

19. Rockman, *Scraping By*, 112–14.

20. Bradford, *Harriet* (1886), 129.

CONCLUSION: THE ROCK

1. Helen Tatlock quoted in Larson, *Bound for the Promised Land*, 80.

2. Bradford, *Harriet* (1886), 42.

3. Keyes, "Harriet Tubman, an Unsung Naturalist."

4. Bradford, *Harriet* (1886), 48.

5. Bryant interview, Oral History Project, Maryland State Parks,

39. Bryant's great-great-grandfather was Tubman's brother. She described her genealogical relationship to Tubman as follows: "Her brother is my great, great grandfather. That's the simple answer." Bryant interview, Oral History Project, Maryland State Parks, 2.

6. Geraldine Copes interview, Oral History Project, Maryland State Parks, November 21, 2011, 13. Copes's grandmother was Tubman's niece. She described her genealogical relationship to Tubman as follows: "Harriet Tubman is my great aunt. Her niece, Mary Elliot, is my grandmother." Copes interview, 1.

7. Horton, *Harriet Tubman*, v.

8. The Harriet Tubman Underground Railroad Visitor Center is operated by the state of Maryland, which leases office space to the National Park Service; the NPS also contributed funding to the development of the site. For more on the Tubman Park Visitor Center exhibit, see Perri Meldon, "Landscape as Witness: Harriet Tubman Underground Railroad State Park," *Black Perspectives*, May 6, 2020, https://www.aaihs.org/landscape-as-witness-harriet-tubman-underground-railroad-state-park-perri-meldon/. Also see Perri Meldon, "Harriet Tubman Underground Railroad State Park, *American Quarterly* 72, no. 4 (December 2020): 979–91.

9. Bryant interview, Oral History Project, Maryland State Parks. The year before Tubman died, Judy Bryant's family planted two trees to mark the graves of Tubman's brother (William Henry Ross Stewart, Sr.), nephew (William H. Stewart, Jr.), and niece-in-law (Emma Moseby Stewart). The baby trees grew together over time, creating the largest tree in the cemetery. Tubman was buried near her relatives and the memorial trees, a fitting symbolism of her life and the value she placed on relationality and interconnection. Kate Larson email to Tiya Miles, July 16, 2023.

10. Drew, *Fugitive Slaves in Canada*, 30.

THE TICKET: A NOTE ON PROCESS AND SOURCES

1. Bradford, *Scenes* (1869), 27–28.

2. Elizabeth Cobbs, *The Tubman Command* (New York: Arcade Publishing, 2019).

3. Alice Walker, "Coming Apart," www.feminist-reprise.org, 100. Walker, *In Search of Our Mothers' Gardens*, xi. Melanie L. Harris, "Ecowomanism: An Introduction," *Worldviews: Global Religions, Culture, and Ecology* 20 (2016): 5–14, 9.

4. Katie Geneva Cannon, "The Emergence of Black Feminist Consciousness," in *Katie's Canon: Womanism and the Soul of the Black Community* (New York: Continuum, 1998), 47–56.

5. Walker, *In Search of Our Mothers' Gardens*, xi. Melanie L. Harris, *Ecowomanism: African American Women and Earth-Honoring Faiths* (2021 reprint; Maryknoll, NY: Orbis Books, 2017), 24. Cannon, *Katie's Canon* (2021), 29. "Godforce" quote: Williams, *Sisters in the Wilderness*, 205, 210.

6. Harris, *Ecowomanism*, 20.

7. Harris, "Ecowomanism: An Introduction," 5–14, 14.

8. I have selected the term and frame of ecowomanism for this study, for reasons described in the text. Another pathway through these gender, Blackness, and ecology questions could be labeled Black feminist environmental thought, which has been advanced by several twentieth-century creative writers and interdisciplinary scholars in the fields of Black studies, feminist studies, American studies, and critical geography. This pathway would include Alice Walker's definition of womanism in *In Search of Our Mothers' Gardens*, as well as other foundational texts like Toni Morrison, "Sites of Memory," in Toni Morrison, *What Moves at the Margin: Selected Nonfiction*, Carolyn C. Denard, ed. (Jackson: University Press of Mississippi, 2008); Katherine McKittrick, *Demonic Grounds:*

Black Women and the Cartographies of Struggle (Minneapolis: University of Minnesota Press, 2006); Glave, *Rooted in the Earth*; Alison H. Deming and Lauret E. Savoy, eds., *The Colors of Nature: Culture, Identity, and the Natural World* (Minneapolis: Milkweed Editions, 2002). More recent works would include Lauret E. Savoy, *Trace: Memory, History, Race, and the American Landscape* (Berkeley: Counterpoint Press, 2016); Kishi Animashaun Ducre, "The Black Feminist Spatial Imagination and an Intersectional Environmental Justice," *Environmental Sociology* 4, no. 1 (2018): 22–35; Tiya Miles, "Structures of Stone and Rings of Light: Spirited Landscapes in Toni Morrison's *Beloved*," in David Carrasco, Stephanie Paulsell, and Mara Willard, eds., *Toni Morrison: Goodness and the Literary Imagination* (Charlottesville: University Press of Virginia, 2019); Cahill, "BlackGirl Geography," 47–62; Alexis Pauline Gumbs, *Undrowned: Black Feminist Lessons from Marine Mammals* (Chico, CA: AK Press, 2020); Chanda Prescod-Weinstein, *The Disordered Cosmos: A Journey into Dark Matter, Spacetime, & Dreams Deferred* (New York: Bold Type Books, 2021); Frances Roberts-Gregory, "Ecowomanist (Auto)Ethnography (EWAE) as Methodological Intervention: BIWOC Everyday Resistance to Louisiana State-Corporate Crime, Anti-Resilient Climate Justice, and Emergent Feminist Abolition Ecologies," PhD dissertation, University of California, Berkeley, 2021. Teona Mercedes Williams, "Deepening Roots: Black Feminist Ecological Practices in the Civil Rights Era, 1940–1990," Order No. 29392552, Yale University, 2022, http://search.proquest.com.ezp-prod1.hul.harvard.edu/dissertations-theses/deepening-roots-black-feminist-ecological/docview/2781503940/se-2; Emily Raboteau, *Lessons for Survival: Mothering Against "the Apocalypse"* (New York: Henry Holt and Company, 2024).

For an overview of themes and authors in the field of Black

feminist environmental thought, or Black feminist ecologies, or Black feminist geographies, or womanist cartographies, see Carlyn Ferrari, "On Black Women's Ecologies," *Black Perspectives*, June 30, 2020, https://www.aaihs.org/on-black-womens-ecologies/; and also see Celeste Henery, "Contemplating Black Ecologies," *Black Perspectives*, May 4, 2021, https://www.aaihs.org/contemplating -black-ecologies/.

For more on the marginalization of Black people in public spaces and in environmental history, see Carolyn Finney, "Who Gets Left Out of the 'Great Outdoors' Story?" *New York Times*, November 4, 2021; Tiya Miles, "Black Bodies, Green Spaces," *New York Times*, June 15, 2019; Carolyn Finney, *Black Faces, White Spaces: Reimagining the Relationship of African Americans to the Great Outdoors* (Chapel Hill: University of North Carolina Press, 2014). For studies of African American environmental history and thought, see Dianne D. Glave and Mark Stoll, eds., *"To Love the Wind and the Rain": African Americans and Environmental History* (Pittsburgh: University of Pittsburgh Press, 2006); Kimberly K. Smith, *African American Environmental Thought: Foundations* (Lawrence: University Press of Kansas, 2007); Tiya Miles, "Haunted Waters: Stories of Slavery, Coastal Ghosts, and Environmental Consciousness," in Paul S. Sutter and Paul M. Pressly, eds., *Coastal Nature, Coastal Culture: Environmental Histories of the Georgia Coast* (Athens: University of Georgia Press, 2018). *Black Ecologies*, a term coined by sociologist Nathan Hare in 1970 and recently revived in African American studies, is a way of categorizing work on African Americans and the environment. Black Ecologies is described by historian J. T. Roane and anthropologist Justin Hosbey as a "corpus of insurgent knowledge" produced by "Black communities in the US South and in the wider African Diaspora . . . most susceptible to the effects of climate change, including rising sea levels, subsidence, sinking land, as well as the ongoing effects of toxic stewardship." For more on Black Ecologies, see Nathan Hare, "Black Ecology," *The Black Scholar* 1, no. 6 (1970): 2–8; J. T. Roane and Justin Hosbey, "Mapping Black Ecologies," *Current Research in Digital History* 2 (August 2019): 2, https://crdh.rrchnm.org /essays/v02-05-mapping-black-ecologies/; J. T. Roane, "Plotting the Black Commons," *Souls: A Critical Journal of Black Politics, Culture and Society* 20, no. 3 (January 2018): 239–66; AAIHS Editors, "Introducing a New Series on Black Ecologies," *Black Perspectives*, June 16, 2020, https://www.aaihs.org/introducing-the-black -ecologies-series/; Tiffany Lethabo King, "The Labor of (Re)reading Plantation Landscapes Fungible(ly)," *Antipode Online* 48, no. 4 (September 2016), https://onlinelibrary.wiley.com/doi/10.1111/anti .12227; Tiffany Lethabo King, "Racial Ecologies: Black Landscapes in Flux," in LeiLani Nishime and Kim D. Hester Williams, eds., *Racial Ecologies* (Seattle: University of Washington Press, 2018).

For recent work on Black environmentalism and justice, see Allison Puglisi, "Redefining Residency: Black Environmental Thought in New Orleans, 1929–1998," PhD dissertation, Harvard University, 2021.

9. Maryland State Wildlife Action Plan, 22.
10. Maryland State Wildlife Action Plan, 12.
11. Martha S. Jones, "Finding Traces of Harriet Tubman on Maryland's Eastern Shore," *New York Times*, June 21, 2022. Perri Meldon, "Tubman's Blackwater: Wading through Public History at a Wildlife Refuge," June 3, 2022, paper accepted for publication, *The Public Historian*.
12. Frederick Douglass to Harriet Tubman, in Bradford, *Harriet* (1886), Appendix 134–35. Also see Horton, *Harriet Tubman*, 143–44.

Index

Page numbers in *italics* refer to photographs.

childhood and teen years of,
xviii, 12, 25, 30, 32–49, 53,
55–65, 68–73, 76–77, 81, 82,
84–87, 89, 90, 94, 95, 147, 231
Civil War work of, xxii, *xxix*,
200–210, 221
in Combahee River Raid, 14,
204–10, *207*
con men and, 219
cradle of, 3, 32–34
daughter adopted by, 216
death of, 222
dreams of, 16–17, 76, 106–16,
120, 123, 127, 132, 144, 196,
197, 200
escapes from slavery, 70, 109,
116, 121–27, *124*, 131–34,
136–47, 150, 186, 234
family history investigated by,
94, 225–26
father of, *see* Ross, Ben
head injury and disability of,
14, 16–17, 69–73, 76–77,
84–86, 88–90, 92, 95–96, 99,
105–7, 150, 178, 224
as healer, 202–3, 211
health care center established
by, 221–22
illnesses of, 105, 117–18,
123, 198
intelligence of, 12–14, 17, 18

marriage to John Tubman,
103–8, 116, 117, 120, 133, 147,
148, 150–52, 155
Moses as name for, xx, 22,
165–66, 169, 172, 206, 208
mother of, *see* Green,
Harriet "Rit"
name of, xviii, 46, 104–6
nieces and nephews of, 121,
133, 148, 156, 200
oxen purchased by, 94
in Philadelphia, 146–48,
151, 186
precognition of, 58,
173–75, 200
as quilter, 136–37, 166
relationships of, 231
remarriage of, 216
siblings of, 36–39, 63–64, 87,
117, 121–26, *124*, 133, 134,
139, 150, 164–66, 187, 225
as slave, xviii, 25, 32, 34, 35,
38–49, 53, 55–65, 68–73, 76–
77, 81, 84–90, 103, 106, 107,
116–18, 120–21, 123, 131
in snowstorm, xv–xx, xxvi,
33, 185
social network of, 219–21,
231–32
toothache suffered by, 177–78
voice of, 131–32